I0009811

CONFIGURING ACCOUNTS PAYABLE WITHIN DYNAMICS 365 FOR OPERATIONS

MODULE 2: **CONFIGURING THE ACCOUNTS PAYABLE VENDOR ACCOUNTS**

Murray Fife

© 2017 Blind Squirrel Publishing, LLC, All Rights Reserved

All Rights Reserved

ISBN-13: 978-1548976583

ISBN-10: 154897658X

DYNAMICS COMPANIONS
BARE BONES CONFIGURATION GUIDE

CONFIGURING ACCOUNTS PAYABLE WITHIN DYNAMICS 365 FOR OPERATIONS
MODULE 2: CONFIGURING THE ACCOUNTS PAYABLE VENDOR ACCOUNTS

Preface

What You Need for this Guide

All the examples shown in this blueprint were done with the Microsoft Dynamics 365 for Operations hosted image that was provisioned through Lifecycle Services.

The following list of software from the virtual image was leveraged within this guide:

Microsoft Dynamics 365 for Operations

Even though all the preceding software was used during the development and testing of the recipes in this book, they should also work on later versions without any changes.

Errata

Although we have taken every care to ensure the accuracy of our content, mistakes do happen. If you find a mistake in one of our books—maybe a mistake in the text or the code—we would be grateful if you would report this to us. By doing so, you can save other readers from frustration and help us improve subsequent versions of this book. If you find any errata, please report them by emailing editor@dynamicscompanions.com.

Piracy

Piracy of copyright material on the Internet is an ongoing problem across all media. If you come across any illegal copies of our works, in any form, on the Internet, please provide us with the location address or website name immediately so that we can pursue a remedy.

Please contact us at legal@dynamicscompanions.com with a link to the suspected pirated material.

We appreciate your help in protecting our authors, and our ability to bring you valuable content.

Questions

You can contact us at help@dynamicscompanions.com if you are having a problem with any aspect of the book, and we will do our best to address it.

 www.dynamicscompanions.com
Dynamics Companions

- 3 -

www.blindsquirrelpublishing.com
© 2017 Blind Squirrel Publishing, LLC, All Rights Reserved

BLIND SQUIRREL
PUBLISHING

DYNAMICS COMPANIONS
BARE BONES CONFIGURATION GUIDE

CONFIGURING ACCOUNTS PAYABLE WITHIN DYNAMICS 365 FOR OPERATIONS
MODULE 2: CONFIGURING THE ACCOUNTS PAYABLE VENDOR ACCOUNTS

www.dynamicscompanions.com
Dynamics Companions

- 4 -

www.blindsquirrelpublishing.com
© 2017 Blind Squirrel Publishing, LLC, All Rights Reserved

BLIND SQUIRREL
PUBLISHING

DYNAMICS COMPANIONS
BARE BONES CONFIGURATION GUIDE

CONFIGURING ACCOUNTS PAYABLE WITHIN DYNAMICS 365 FOR OPERATIONS
MODULE 2: CONFIGURING THE ACCOUNTS PAYABLE VENDOR ACCOUNTS

Table of Contents

dync
dynamics companions
www.dynamicscompanions.com
Dynamics Companions

- 5 -

www.blindsquirrelpublishing.com
© 2017 Blind Squirrel Publishing, LLC, All Rights Reserved

BLIND SQUIRREL
PUBLISHING

DYNAMICS COMPANIONS
BARE BONES CONFIGURATION GUIDE

CONFIGURING ACCOUNTS PAYABLE WITHIN DYNAMICS 365 FOR OPERATIONS
MODULE 2: CONFIGURING THE ACCOUNTS PAYABLE VENDOR ACCOUNTS

 www.dynamicscompanions.com
Dynamics Companions

- 7 -

www.blindsquirrelpublishing.com
© 2017 Blind Squirrel Publishing, LLC, All Rights Reserved

BLIND SQUIRREL
PUBLISHING

DYNAMICS COMPANIONS
BARE BONES CONFIGURATION GUIDE

CONFIGURING ACCOUNTS PAYABLE WITHIN DYNAMICS 365 FOR OPERATIONS
MODULE 2: CONFIGURING THE ACCOUNTS PAYABLE VENDOR ACCOUNTS

Introduction

Now that you have all of the codes and controls configured you can start adding some real data into the Accounts payable, and the best place to start is by setting up your vendors.

In this guide we will show you how you can set up individual vendors, and also how you can load in all of your vendors in bulk through the Excel integration.

Topics Covered

- Changing the Vendor Numbering Sequence
- Configuring Vendor Groups
- Creating A New Vendor Account
- Importing Vendors Using the Excel Workbook Designer
- Populating and publishing the Import Template
- Updating Vendor Information Manually
- Performing Bulk Updates Using the Grid Editing Feature
- Performing Mass Updates Using Excel

DYNAMICS COMPANIONS
BARE BONES CONFIGURATION GUIDE

CONFIGURING ACCOUNTS PAYABLE WITHIN DYNAMICS 365 FOR OPERATIONS
MODULE 2: CONFIGURING THE ACCOUNTS PAYABLE VENDOR ACCOUNTS

Changing the Vendor Numbering Sequence

Before we start though we will make one quick tweak to the system to allow us to use manual numbering for the vendor accounts. You don't have to do this and can have Dynamics AX assign vendor numbers for you automatically, but if you are like most companies you may want to add some of your own intelligence to the numbering format se we need to make the vendor numbering a little more flexible.

How to do it...

Step 1: Open the Accounts payable parameters form

Navigate to Accounts Payable > Setup > Accounts payable parameters

Step 2: Switch to the Number sequences page

From here we will want to switch to the number sequence details tab.

Click on the **Number sequences** tab

Step 3: View the Vendor account details

We will want to access the **Vendor account** number sequence to make a small change to it.

Right-mouse-click on the **Vendor Account** number sequence, and select **View Details.**

Step 4: Remove unwanted segments

We like to have a simpler format for our vendor account number so we will remove some of them.

Select the **Company** and **Constant** segments and click on the **Remove** button.

Step 5: Set the Manual flag

The final thing that we will want to do here is to set the number sequence to manual so that we can enter in the Vendor numbers without having them automatically created.

Check the **Manual** flag

 www.dynamicscompanions.com
Dynamics Companions

- 9 -

www.blindsquirrelpublishing.com
© 2017 Blind Squirrel Publishing, LLC , All Rights Reserved

BLIND SQUIRREL
PUBLISHING

DYNAMICS COMPANIONS
BARE BONES CONFIGURATION GUIDE

CONFIGURING ACCOUNTS PAYABLE WITHIN DYNAMICS 365 FOR OPERATIONS
MODULE 2: CONFIGURING THE ACCOUNTS PAYABLE VENDOR ACCOUNTS

Changing the Vendor Numbering Sequence

How to do it...

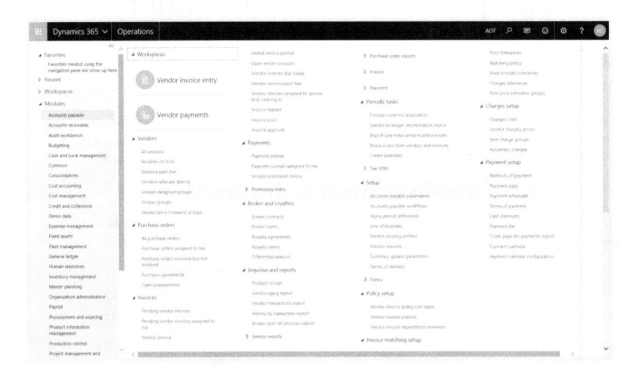

Step 1: Open the Accounts payable parameters form

To make this change we will need to access the accounts payable parameters form.

To do this, open up the navigation panel, expand out the **Modules** group, and click on **Accounts payable** module to see all of the menu items that are available. Then click on the **Accounts payable parameters** menu item within the **Setup** menu group.

dyn_c   www.dynamicscompanions.com
Dynamics Companions

- 10 -

www.blindsquirrelpublishing.com
© 2017 Blind Squirrel Publishing, LLC, All Rights Reserved

BLIND SQUIRREL
PUBLISHING

DYNAMICS COMPANIONS
BARE BONES CONFIGURATION GUIDE

CONFIGURING ACCOUNTS PAYABLE WITHIN DYNAMICS 365 FOR OPERATIONS
MODULE 2: CONFIGURING THE ACCOUNTS PAYABLE VENDOR ACCOUNTS

Changing the Vendor Numbering Sequence

How to do it...

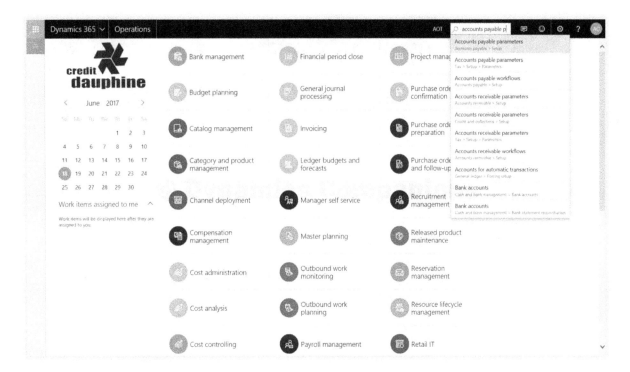

Step 1: Open the Accounts payable parameters form

Alternatively, you can search for the **Accounts payable parameters** form by clicking on the search icon in the header of the form (or press **ALT+G**) and then type in **accounts payable p** into the search box. Then you will be able to select the **Accounts payable parameters** maintenance form from the dropdown list.

dyn c
www.dynamicscompanions.com
Dynamics Companions

- 11 -

www.blindsquirrelpublishing.com
© 2017 Blind Squirrel Publishing, LLC, All Rights Reserved

BLIND SQUIRREL
PUBLISHING

DYNAMICS COMPANIONS
BARE BONES CONFIGURATION GUIDE

CONFIGURING ACCOUNTS PAYABLE WITHIN DYNAMICS 365 FOR OPERATIONS
MODULE 2: CONFIGURING THE ACCOUNTS PAYABLE VENDOR ACCOUNTS

Changing the Vendor Numbering Sequence

How to do it...

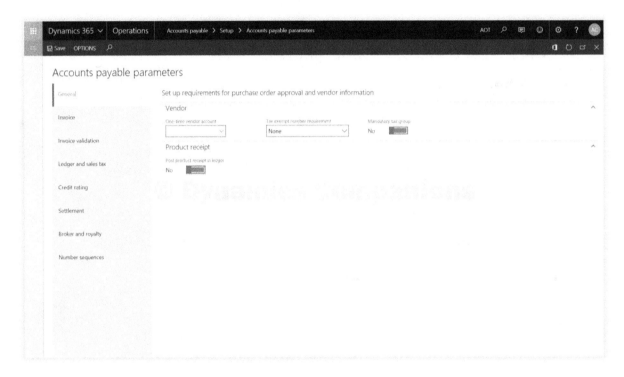

Step 1: Open the Accounts payable parameters form

This will open up the **Accounts payable parameters** form.

www.dynamicscompanions.com
Dynamics Companions

- 12 -

www.blindsquirrelpublishing.com
© 2017 Blind Squirrel Publishing, LLC, All Rights Reserved

BLIND SQUIRREL
PUBLISHING

DYNAMICS COMPANIONS
BARE BONES CONFIGURATION GUIDE

CONFIGURING ACCOUNTS PAYABLE WITHIN DYNAMICS 365 FOR OPERATIONS
MODULE 2: CONFIGURING THE ACCOUNTS PAYABLE VENDOR ACCOUNTS

Changing the Vendor Numbering Sequence

How to do it...

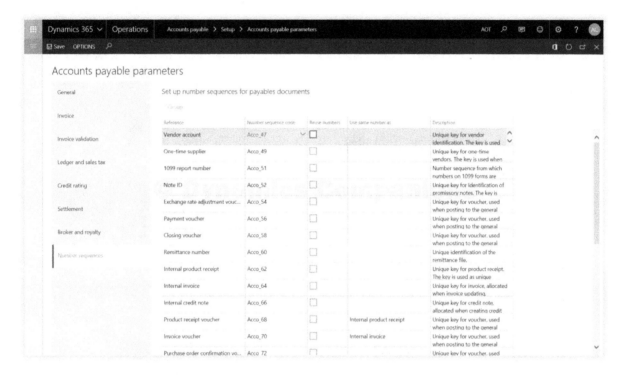

Step 2: Switch to the Number sequences page

From here we will want to switch to the number sequence details tab.

To do this, switch to the **Number Sequences** page.

dyn⊂
www.dynamicscompanions.com
Dynamics Companions

- 13 -

www.blindsquirrelpublishing.com
© 2017 Blind Squirrel Publishing, LLC, All Rights Reserved

BLIND SQUIRREL
PUBLISHING

DYNAMICS COMPANIONS
BARE BONES CONFIGURATION GUIDE

CONFIGURING ACCOUNTS PAYABLE WITHIN DYNAMICS 365 FOR OPERATIONS
MODULE 2: CONFIGURING THE ACCOUNTS PAYABLE VENDOR ACCOUNTS

Changing the Vendor Numbering Sequence

How to do it...

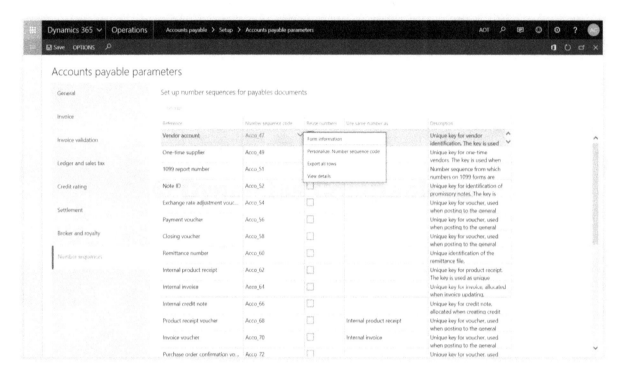

Step 3: View the Vendor account details

This page will show us all of the **Number sequences** that are used within the **Accounts Payable** module.

We will want to access the **Vendor account** number sequence to make a small change to it.

To do this, right-mouse-click on the **Vendor Account** number sequence, and click on the **View Details** menu item.

dync
www.dynamicscompanions.com
Dynamics Companions

- 14 -

www.blindsquirrelpublishing.com
© 2017 Blind Squirrel Publishing, LLC, All Rights Reserved

BLIND SQUIRREL
PUBLISHING

DYNAMICS COMPANIONS
BARE BONES CONFIGURATION GUIDE

CONFIGURING ACCOUNTS PAYABLE WITHIN DYNAMICS 365 FOR OPERATIONS
MODULE 2: CONFIGURING THE ACCOUNTS PAYABLE VENDOR ACCOUNTS

Changing the Vendor Numbering Sequence

How to do it...

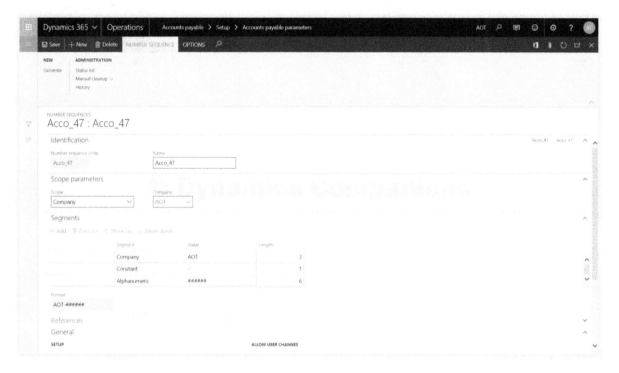

Step 3: View the Vendor account details

This will open up the Number sequence for the **Vendors** where we can make our small change.

www.dynamicscompanions.com
Dynamics Companions

- 15 -

www.blindsquirrelpublishing.com
© 2017 Blind Squirrel Publishing, LLC, All Rights Reserved

BLIND SQUIRREL
PUBLISHING

DYNAMICS COMPANIONS
BARE BONES CONFIGURATION GUIDE

CONFIGURING ACCOUNTS PAYABLE WITHIN DYNAMICS 365 FOR OPERATIONS
MODULE 2: CONFIGURING THE ACCOUNTS PAYABLE VENDOR ACCOUNTS

Changing the Vendor Numbering Sequence

How to do it...

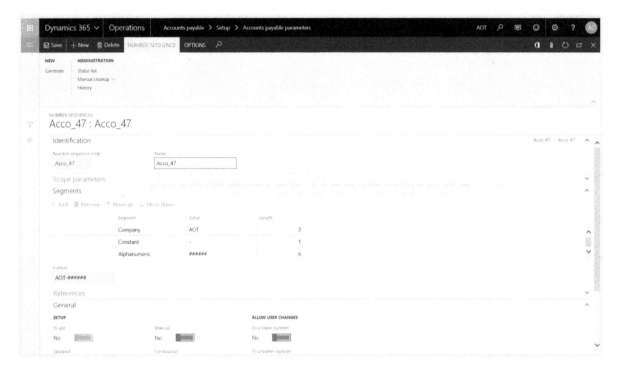

Step 4: Remove unwanted segments

By default, the vendor number includes the company code and also a constant.

We like to have a simpler format for our vendor account number so we will remove some of them.

To do this, we just select the segments that we don't want to use and then click on the **Remove** button.

Here we will select the **Company** and **Constant** segments and click the **Remove** button for each of them so that your vendor number format just a numeric value.

dyn c
www.dynamicscompanions.com
Dynamics Companions

- 16 -

www.blindsquirrelpublishing.com
© 2017 Blind Squirrel Publishing, LLC, All Rights Reserved

BLIND SQUIRREL
PUBLISHING

DYNAMICS COMPANIONS
BARE BONES CONFIGURATION GUIDE

CONFIGURING ACCOUNTS PAYABLE WITHIN DYNAMICS 365 FOR OPERATIONS
MODULE 2: CONFIGURING THE ACCOUNTS PAYABLE VENDOR ACCOUNTS

Changing the Vendor Numbering Sequence

How to do it...

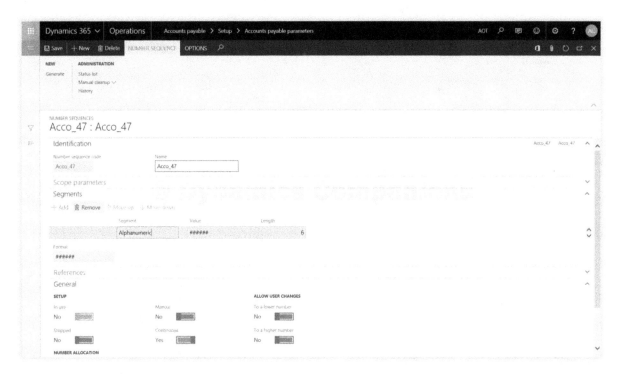

Step 4: Remove unwanted segments

After we have done that our number sequence segments will look a lot cleaner.

dyn c
www.dynamicscompanions.com
Dynamics Companions

- 17 -

www.blindsquirrelpublishing.com
© 2017 Blind Squirrel Publishing, LLC, All Rights Reserved

BLIND SQUIRREL
PUBLISHING

DYNAMICS COMPANIONS
BARE BONES CONFIGURATION GUIDE

CONFIGURING ACCOUNTS PAYABLE WITHIN DYNAMICS 365 FOR OPERATIONS
MODULE 2: CONFIGURING THE ACCOUNTS PAYABLE VENDOR ACCOUNTS

Changing the Vendor Numbering Sequence

How to do it...

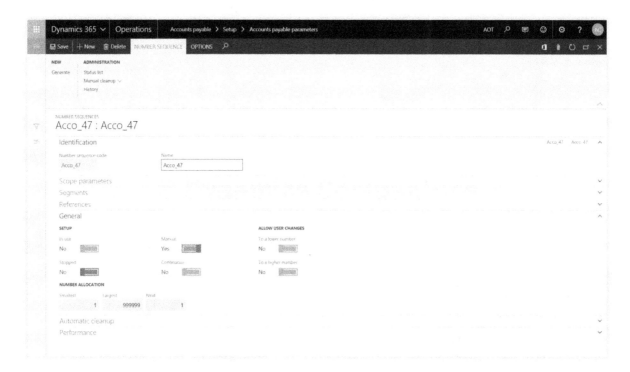

Step 5: Set the Manual flag

The final thing that we will want to do here is to set the number sequence to manual so that we can enter in the Vendor numbers without having them automatically created.

To do this, just check the **Manual** flag within the **General** tab group.

After you have done that you can just click on the **Close** button to exit from the form.

dync
www.dynamicscompanions.com
Dynamics Companions

- 18 -

www.blindsquirrelpublishing.com
© 2017 Blind Squirrel Publishing, LLC, All Rights Reserved

BLIND SQUIRREL
PUBLISHING

DYNAMICS COMPANIONS
BARE BONES CONFIGURATION GUIDE

CONFIGURING ACCOUNTS PAYABLE WITHIN DYNAMICS 365 FOR OPERATIONS
MODULE 2: CONFIGURING THE ACCOUNTS PAYABLE VENDOR ACCOUNTS

Changing the Vendor Numbering Sequence

Example Data

Field Name	Value
Segment.Alphanumeric	######
Manual	True

Number Sequence: Vendor Account

dyn℮
www.dynamicscompanions.com
Dynamics Companions

- 19 -

www.blindsquirrelpublishing.com
© 2017 Blind Squirrel Publishing, LLC, All Rights Reserved

BLIND SQUIRREL
PUBLISHING

DYNAMICS COMPANIONS
BARE BONES CONFIGURATION GUIDE

CONFIGURING ACCOUNTS PAYABLE WITHIN DYNAMICS 365 FOR OPERATIONS
MODULE 2: CONFIGURING THE ACCOUNTS PAYABLE VENDOR ACCOUNTS

Changing the Vendor Numbering Sequence

Review

This may seem like a small change to make within the system, but changing the number sequence for the **Vendor** account is a great trick to have in our back pocket. If we want to add any control to the vendor numbering then we can tweak the number sequence to have more elements, or if we want the numbering to be a little more free-form then we can do just what we did here and let us choose the number ourselves.

DYNAMICS COMPANIONS
BARE BONES CONFIGURATION GUIDE

CONFIGURING ACCOUNTS PAYABLE WITHIN DYNAMICS 365 FOR OPERATIONS
MODULE 2: CONFIGURING THE ACCOUNTS PAYABLE VENDOR ACCOUNTS

Configuring Vendor Groups

Before we set up the vendors we need to set up some **Vendor Groups** that you will use to classify your vendors.

How to do it...

Step 1: Open the Vendor groups form

To make this change we will need to access the **Vendor groups** form.

Navigate to Accounts Payable > Vendors > Vendor groups

Step 2: Click New

Now we want to set up some default groups for our vendors.

Click on the **+ New** button

Step 3: Type in a Vendor group

Now we will be able to give it a vendor group code.

Set the Vendor group to PARTS.

Step 4: Type in a Description

Now we will want to give our Vendor group a better description to explain its use..

Set the Description to Parts Vendors.

Step 5: Set the default Terms of payment

Now we will want to specify is the default **Terms of payment** for the vendor group.

Set the Terms of payment to NET30.

Step 6: Repeat for other Vendor groups

Now we will create a **Vendor group** for our service providers.

Click on the **New** button and enter the Vendor group details.

Next we will create a **Vendor group** for our intercompany vendors.

Click on the **New** button and enter the Vendor group details.

Now we will add a **Vendor group** to track our tax authorities.

Click on the **New** button and enter the Vendor group details.

Finally we will create a new **Vendor group** to track all of the other vendors that don't fit into any of our main groups.

Click on the **New** button and enter the Vendor group details.

www.dynamicscompanions.com
Dynamics Companions

- 21 -

www.blindsquirrelpublishing.com
© 2017 Blind Squirrel Publishing, LLC, All Rights Reserved

BLIND SQUIRREL
PUBLISHING

DYNAMICS COMPANIONS
BARE BONES CONFIGURATION GUIDE

CONFIGURING ACCOUNTS PAYABLE WITHIN DYNAMICS 365 FOR OPERATIONS
MODULE 2: CONFIGURING THE ACCOUNTS PAYABLE VENDOR ACCOUNTS

Configuring Vendor Groups

How to do it...

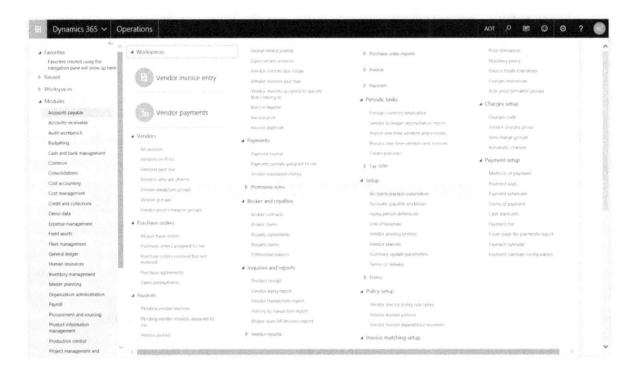

Step 1: Open the Vendor groups form

To make this change we will need to access the **Vendor groups** form.

To do this, open up the navigation panel, expand out the **Modules** group, and click on **Accounts payable** module to see all of the menu items that are available. Then click on the **Vendor groups** menu item within the **Vendor** menu group.

dyn_c   www.dynamicscompanions.com
Dynamics Companions

- 22 -

www.blindsquirrelpublishing.com
© 2017 Blind Squirrel Publishing, LLC, All Rights Reserved

BLIND SQUIRREL
PUBLISHING

DYNAMICS COMPANIONS
BARE BONES CONFIGURATION GUIDE

CONFIGURING ACCOUNTS PAYABLE WITHIN DYNAMICS 365 FOR OPERATIONS
MODULE 2: CONFIGURING THE ACCOUNTS PAYABLE VENDOR ACCOUNTS

Configuring Vendor Groups

How to do it...

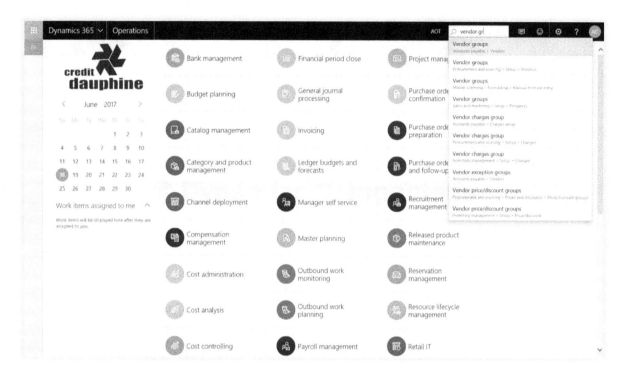

Step 1: Open the Vendor groups form

Alternatively, you can search for the **Vendor groups** form by clicking on the search icon in the header of the form (or press **ALT+G**) and then type in **vendor gr** into the search box. Then you will be able to select the **Vendor groups** maintenance form from the dropdown list.

dync

www.dynamicscompanions.com
Dynamics Companions

- 23 -

www.blindsquirrelpublishing.com
© 2017 Blind Squirrel Publishing, LLC, All Rights Reserved

BLIND SQUIRREL
PUBLISHING

DYNAMICS COMPANIONS
BARE BONES CONFIGURATION GUIDE

CONFIGURING ACCOUNTS PAYABLE WITHIN DYNAMICS 365 FOR OPERATIONS
MODULE 2: CONFIGURING THE ACCOUNTS PAYABLE VENDOR ACCOUNTS

Configuring Vendor Groups

How to do it...

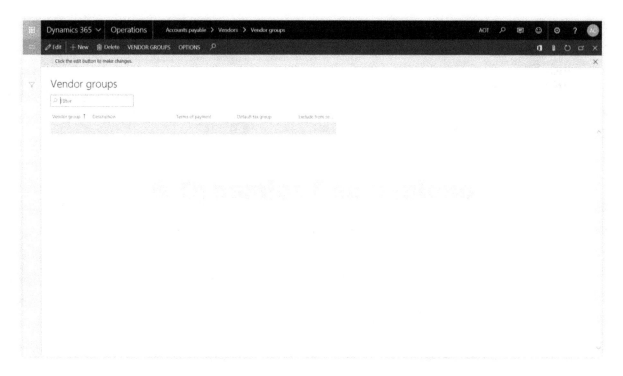

Step 1: Open the Vendor groups form

This will open up the **Vendor groups** form.

dync
www.dynamicscompanions.com
Dynamics Companions

- 24 -

www.blindsquirrelpublishing.com
© 2017 Blind Squirrel Publishing, LLC, All Rights Reserved

BLIND SQUIRREL
PUBLISHING

DYNAMICS COMPANIONS
BARE BONES CONFIGURATION GUIDE

CONFIGURING ACCOUNTS PAYABLE WITHIN DYNAMICS 365 FOR OPERATIONS
MODULE 2: CONFIGURING THE ACCOUNTS PAYABLE VENDOR ACCOUNTS

Configuring Vendor Groups

How to do it...

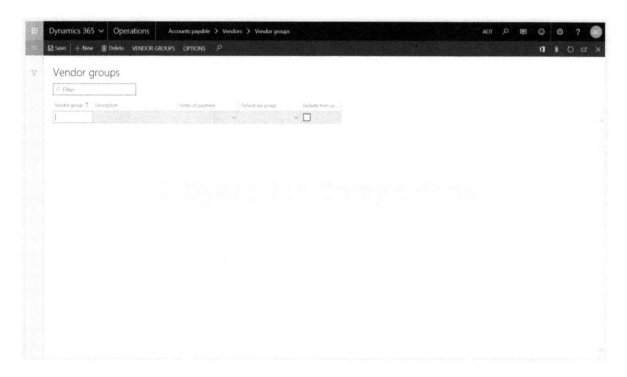

Step 2: Click New

Now we want to set up some default groups for our vendors.

To do this, click on the **New** button in the menu bar to create a new record.

www.dynamicscompanions.com
Dynamics Companions

- 25 -

www.blindsquirrelpublishing.com
© 2017 Blind Squirrel Publishing, LLC , All Rights Reserved

BLIND SQUIRREL
PUBLISHING

DYNAMICS COMPANIONS
BARE BONES CONFIGURATION GUIDE

CONFIGURING ACCOUNTS PAYABLE WITHIN DYNAMICS 365 FOR OPERATIONS
MODULE 2: CONFIGURING THE ACCOUNTS PAYABLE VENDOR ACCOUNTS

Configuring Vendor Groups

How to do it...

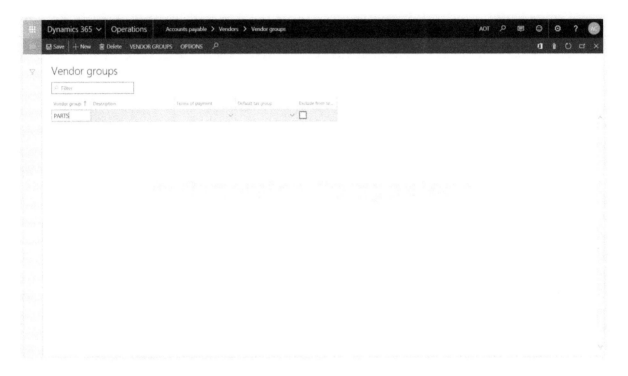

Step 3: Type in a Vendor group

This will create a new **Vendor group** record for us.

Now we will be able to give it a vendor group code.

To do this, enter in the code into the **Vendor Group** field.

For this record we will set the **Vendor group** to **PARTS.**

www.dynamicscompanions.com
Dynamics Companions

- 26 -

www.blindsquirrelpublishing.com
© 2017 Blind Squirrel Publishing, LLC, All Rights Reserved

BLIND SQUIRREL
PUBLISHING

DYNAMICS COMPANIONS
BARE BONES CONFIGURATION GUIDE

CONFIGURING ACCOUNTS PAYABLE WITHIN DYNAMICS 365 FOR OPERATIONS
MODULE 2: CONFIGURING THE ACCOUNTS PAYABLE VENDOR ACCOUNTS

Configuring Vendor Groups

How to do it...

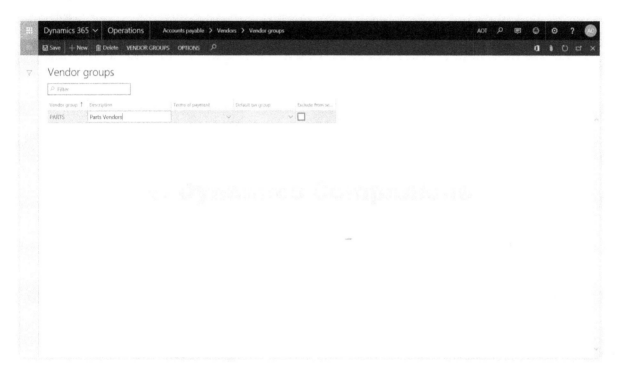

Step 4: Type in a Description

Now we will want to give our Vendor group a better description to explain its use..

To do this, just type in a more detailed explanation of the vendor group into the **Description** field.

For this Vendor group we will set the **Description** to **Parts Vendors**.

dyn c
Dynamics Companions

www.dynamicscompanions.com
Dynamics Companions

- 27 -

www.blindsquirrelpublishing.com
© 2017 Blind Squirrel Publishing, LLC, All Rights Reserved

BLIND SQUIRREL
PUBLISHING

DYNAMICS COMPANIONS
BARE BONES CONFIGURATION GUIDE

CONFIGURING ACCOUNTS PAYABLE WITHIN DYNAMICS 365 FOR OPERATIONS
MODULE 2: CONFIGURING THE ACCOUNTS PAYABLE VENDOR ACCOUNTS

Configuring Vendor Groups

How to do it...

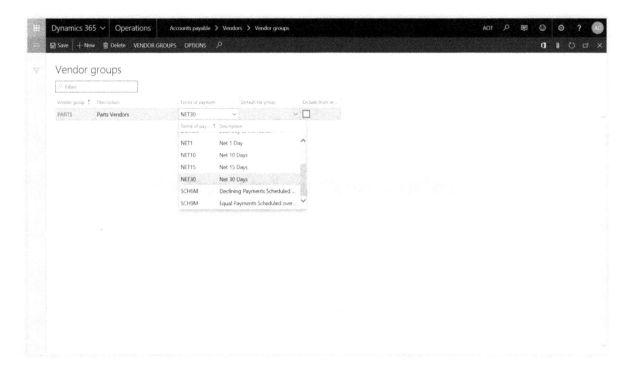

Step 5: Set the default Terms of payment

The **Vendor group** is not just for classifying and grouping the vendors, it also allows us to set some default codes to use when the vendor is assigned to the group.

Now we will want to specify is the default **Terms of payment** for the vendor group.

To do this, click on the **Terms Of Payment** drop-down list, and select the default Terms of payment code from the list.

For this record we will set the **Terms of payment** to **NET30.**

After we have done that our **Vendor group** will be configured.

dync
www.dynamicscompanions.com
Dynamics Companions

- 28 -

www.blindsquirrelpublishing.com
© 2017 Blind Squirrel Publishing, LLC, All Rights Reserved

BLIND SQUIRREL
PUBLISHING

DYNAMICS COMPANIONS
BARE BONES CONFIGURATION GUIDE

CONFIGURING ACCOUNTS PAYABLE WITHIN DYNAMICS 365 FOR OPERATIONS
MODULE 2: CONFIGURING THE ACCOUNTS PAYABLE VENDOR ACCOUNTS

Configuring Vendor Groups

How to do it...

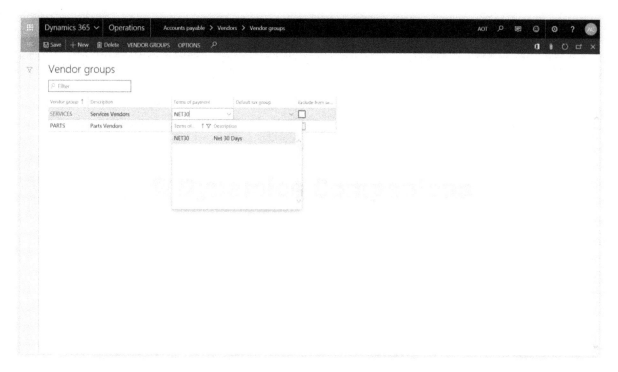

Step 6: Repeat for other Vendor groups

We can repeat this process for all of the different groups that you want to use to classify your vendors.

Now we will create a **Vendor group** for our service providers.

To do this, just click **New** again and enter in the vendor group details.

For this Vendor group we will set the Vendor group to SERVICES, the Description to Service vendors, and the Terms of payment to NET30.

dyn⊆
www.dynamicscompanions.com
Dynamics Companions

- 29 -

www.blindsquirrelpublishing.com
© 2017 Blind Squirrel Publishing, LLC , All Rights Reserved

BLIND SQUIRREL
PUBLISHING

DYNAMICS COMPANIONS
BARE BONES CONFIGURATION GUIDE

CONFIGURING ACCOUNTS PAYABLE WITHIN DYNAMICS 365 FOR OPERATIONS
MODULE 2: CONFIGURING THE ACCOUNTS PAYABLE VENDOR ACCOUNTS

Configuring Vendor Groups

How to do it...

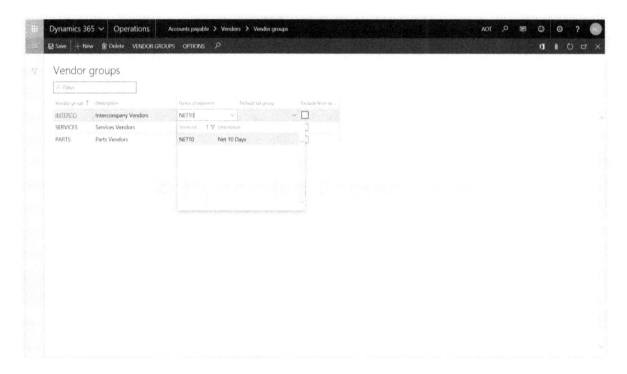

Step 6: Repeat for other Vendor groups

Next we will create a **Vendor group** for our intercompany vendors.

To do this, just click **New** again and enter in the vendor group details.

For this Vendor group we will set the Vendor group to INTERCO, the Description to Intercompany vendors, and the Terms of payment to NET10.

www.blindsquirrelpublishing.com
© 2017 Blind Squirrel Publishing, LLC, All Rights Reserved

BLIND SQUIRREL
PUBLISHING

DYNAMICS COMPANIONS
BARE BONES CONFIGURATION GUIDE

CONFIGURING ACCOUNTS PAYABLE WITHIN DYNAMICS 365 FOR OPERATIONS
MODULE 2: CONFIGURING THE ACCOUNTS PAYABLE VENDOR ACCOUNTS

Configuring Vendor Groups

How to do it...

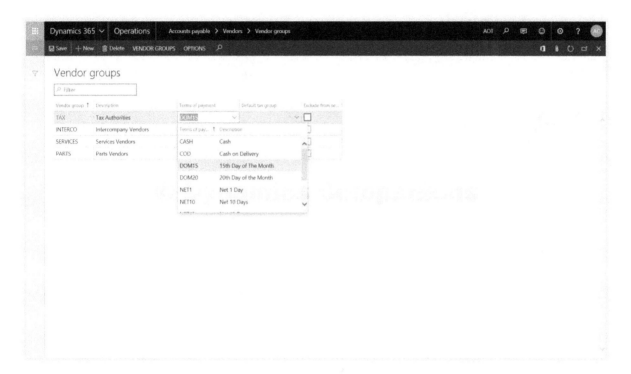

Step 6: Repeat for other Vendor groups

Now we will add a **Vendor group** to track our tax authorities.

To do this, just click **New** again and enter in the vendor group details.

For this Vendor group we will set the Vendor group to TAX, the Description to Tax authorities, and the Terms of payment to DOM15.

dyn c
www.dynamicscompanions.com
Dynamics Companions

- 31 -

www.blindsquirrelpublishing.com
© 2017 Blind Squirrel Publishing, LLC , All Rights Reserved

BLIND SQUIRREL
PUBLISHING

DYNAMICS COMPANIONS
BARE BONES CONFIGURATION GUIDE

CONFIGURING ACCOUNTS PAYABLE WITHIN DYNAMICS 365 FOR OPERATIONS
MODULE 2: CONFIGURING THE ACCOUNTS PAYABLE VENDOR ACCOUNTS

Configuring Vendor Groups

How to do it...

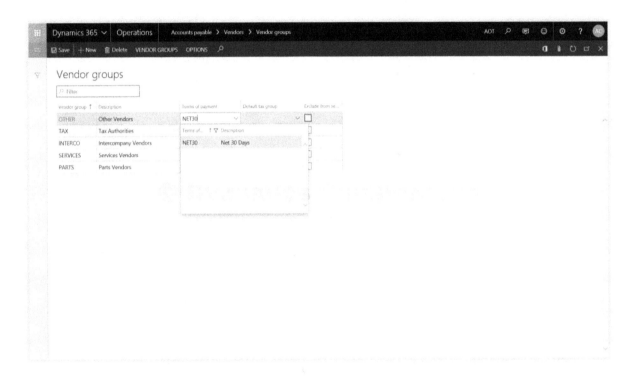

Step 6: Repeat for other Vendor groups

Finally we will create a new **Vendor group** to track all of the other vendors that don't fit into any of our main groups.

To do this, just click **New** again and enter in the vendor group details.

For this Vendor group we will set the Vendor group to OTHER, the Description to Other vendors, and the Terms of payment to NET30.

DYNAMICS COMPANIONS
BARE BONES CONFIGURATION GUIDE

CONFIGURING ACCOUNTS PAYABLE WITHIN DYNAMICS 365 FOR OPERATIONS
MODULE 2: CONFIGURING THE ACCOUNTS PAYABLE VENDOR ACCOUNTS

Configuring Vendor Groups

How to do it...

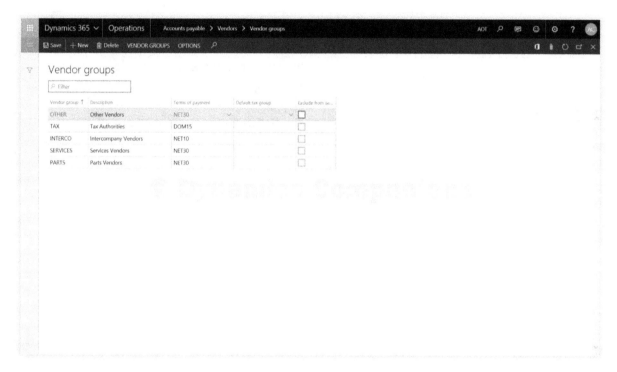

Step 6: Repeat for other Vendor groups

When we are done we can click the **Close** button to exit from the form.

www.dynamicscompanions.com
Dynamics Companions

- 33 -

www.blindsquirrelpublishing.com
© 2017 Blind Squirrel Publishing, LLC, All Rights Reserved

BLIND SQUIRREL
PUBLISHING

DYNAMICS COMPANIONS
BARE BONES CONFIGURATION GUIDE

CONFIGURING ACCOUNTS PAYABLE WITHIN DYNAMICS 365 FOR OPERATIONS
MODULE 2: CONFIGURING THE ACCOUNTS PAYABLE VENDOR ACCOUNTS

Configuring Vendor Groups

Example Data

Field Name	Value
Vendor Group	INTERCO
Description	Intercompany Vendors
Terms of Payment	NET10
Settle Period	NET10

Vendor Group: INTERCO – Intercompany Vendors

www.dynamicscompanions.com
Dynamics Companions

- 34 -

www.blindsquirrelpublishing.com
© 2017 Blind Squirrel Publishing, LLC, All Rights Reserved

BLIND SQUIRREL
PUBLISHING

DYNAMICS COMPANIONS
BARE BONES CONFIGURATION GUIDE

CONFIGURING ACCOUNTS PAYABLE WITHIN DYNAMICS 365 FOR OPERATIONS
MODULE 2: CONFIGURING THE ACCOUNTS PAYABLE VENDOR ACCOUNTS

Configuring Vendor Groups

Example Data

Field Name	Value
Vendor Group	OTHER
Description	Other Vendors
Terms of Payment	NET30
Settle Period	NET10

Vendor Group: OTHER – Other Vendors

dyn c   www.dynamicscompanions.com
Dynamics Companions

- 35 -

www.blindsquirrelpublishing.com
© 2017 Blind Squirrel Publishing, LLC, All Rights Reserved

BLIND SQUIRREL
PUBLISHING

DYNAMICS COMPANIONS
BARE BONES CONFIGURATION GUIDE

CONFIGURING ACCOUNTS PAYABLE WITHIN DYNAMICS 365 FOR OPERATIONS
MODULE 2: CONFIGURING THE ACCOUNTS PAYABLE VENDOR ACCOUNTS

Configuring Vendor Groups

Example Data

Field Name	Value
Vendor Group	PARTS
Description	Parts Vendors
Terms of Payment	NET30
Settle Period	NET10

Vendor Group: PARTS – Parts Vendors

www.dynamicscompanions.com
Dynamics Companions

- 36 -

www.blindsquirrelpublishing.com
© 2017 Blind Squirrel Publishing, LLC, All Rights Reserved

BLIND SQUIRREL
PUBLISHING

DYNAMICS COMPANIONS
BARE BONES CONFIGURATION GUIDE

CONFIGURING ACCOUNTS PAYABLE WITHIN DYNAMICS 365 FOR OPERATIONS
MODULE 2: CONFIGURING THE ACCOUNTS PAYABLE VENDOR ACCOUNTS

Configuring Vendor Groups

Example Data

Field Name	Value
Vendor Group	SERVICES
Description	Services Vendors
Terms of Payment	NET30
Settle Period	NET10

Vendor Group: SERVICES – Services Vendors

dyn c
www.dynamicscompanions.com
Dynamics Companions

- 37 -

www.blindsquirrelpublishing.com
© 2017 Blind Squirrel Publishing, LLC, All Rights Reserved

BLIND SQUIRREL
PUBLISHING

DYNAMICS COMPANIONS
BARE BONES CONFIGURATION GUIDE

CONFIGURING ACCOUNTS PAYABLE WITHIN DYNAMICS 365 FOR OPERATIONS
MODULE 2: CONFIGURING THE ACCOUNTS PAYABLE VENDOR ACCOUNTS

Configuring Vendor Groups

Example Data

Field Name	Value
Vendor Group	TAX
Description	Tax Authorities
Terms of Payment	DOM15
Settle Period	NET10

Vendor Group: TAX – Tax Authorities

DYNAMICS COMPANIONS
BARE BONES CONFIGURATION GUIDE

CONFIGURING ACCOUNTS PAYABLE WITHIN DYNAMICS 365 FOR OPERATIONS
MODULE 2: CONFIGURING THE ACCOUNTS PAYABLE VENDOR ACCOUNTS

Configuring Vendor Groups

Review

Great. Now we have a couple of different ways that we can classify and group our vendors.

www.dynamicscompanions.com
Dynamics Companions

- 39 -

www.blindsquirrelpublishing.com
© 2017 Blind Squirrel Publishing, LLC, All Rights Reserved

BLIND SQUIRREL
PUBLISHING

DYNAMICS COMPANIONS
BARE BONES CONFIGURATION GUIDE

CONFIGURING ACCOUNTS PAYABLE WITHIN DYNAMICS 365 FOR OPERATIONS
MODULE 2: CONFIGURING THE ACCOUNTS PAYABLE VENDOR ACCOUNTS

Creating A New Vendor Account

Now we can start adding our vendors.

How to do it...

Step 1: Open the All vendors form

To make this change we will need to go to the **All vendors** form.

Navigate to Accounts Payable > Vendors > All Vendors

Step 2: Click New

So now we will want to create our first **Vendor** record.

Click on the **+ New** button

Step 3: Select the Record type

By default the record type is **Organization** but if we want to create a vendor that is an person then we will want to change the **Record type** of the **Vendor**.

Click on the **Record type** and select **Person**

Step 4: Change the Record type to Organization

But If our **Vendor** is a company rather than an individual we will want to have the information that shows be more company specific.

Change the Record type to Organization and set

Step 5: Set the Vendor account code

We will start this off by assigning our **Vendor** a **Vendor account** code.

Set the Vendor account code

Step 6: Set the vendor Name

Next we will want to give our vendor a **Name** make them easier to search for.

Set the Name to Tyrell Corporation

Step 7: Select the vendor Group

Next we will want to assign our **Vendor** to a **Vendor Group**.

Set the Group to SERVICES

Step 8: Click on the Add button within the Addresses group

Now we will want to set up an address for our vendor.

Click on the **+Add** button within the **Addresses** groups menu bar.

Step 9: Set the Name or description

Now we will want to assign the **Address** name that we can easily locate it with.

Set the Name or description to Tyrell Corporation

Step 10: Enter in a Zip/postal code

Next we will want to specify the **Zip/Postal code** for the address

Set the Zip/Postal code to 94507

 www.dynamicscompanions.com
Dynamics Companions

- 40 -

www.blindsquirrelpublishing.com
© 2017 Blind Squirrel Publishing, LLC, All Rights Reserved

BLIND SQUIRREL
PUBLISHING

DYNAMICS COMPANIONS
BARE BONES CONFIGURATION GUIDE

CONFIGURING ACCOUNTS PAYABLE WITHIN DYNAMICS 365 FOR OPERATIONS
MODULE 2: CONFIGURING THE ACCOUNTS PAYABLE VENDOR ACCOUNTS

Step 11: Enter in the Street

Next we will want specify the **Street** address for the vendor.

Set the Street to 68 Crest Ave.

Step 12: Click Add within the Contact information

Now we will want to add some contact information for our vendor.

Click on the **+Add** button within the **Contact information** groups menu bar

Step 13: Enter a Description

We will want to start by giving our contact record a description to identify it.

Enter a **Description** for the contact item

Step 14: Select the contact information Type

Now we will want to specify the type of contact information that this record is associated with – i.e. **Phone, e-Mail, URL** etc.

Click on the **Type** drop-down list and select the **Phone** option.

Step 15: Enter in the Contact number/address

Now we will want to enter in the contact number or email address for the contact record.

Set the Contact number/address: to (555) 283-3867

Step 16: Set the Primary flag

Finally, we may want to flag the contact information as the primary contact method for that specific type of contact.

Check the **Primary** check box

Step 17: Expand the Payments tab group

Now we will want to configure some of the payment defaults for the vendor.

Expand the **Payments** tab group

Step 18: Set the default Method of payment

Now we will want to set the default way that we will want to pay the vendor by specifying the **Method of payment.**

Click on the **Method of payment** and select the **CHECK** option

www.dynamicscompanions.com
Dynamics Companions

- 41 -

www.blindsquirrelpublishing.com
© 2017 Blind Squirrel Publishing, LLC, All Rights Reserved

BLIND SQUIRREL
PUBLISHING

DYNAMICS COMPANIONS
BARE BONES CONFIGURATION GUIDE

CONFIGURING ACCOUNTS PAYABLE WITHIN DYNAMICS 365 FOR OPERATIONS
MODULE 2: CONFIGURING THE ACCOUNTS PAYABLE VENDOR ACCOUNTS

Creating A New Vendor Account

How to do it...

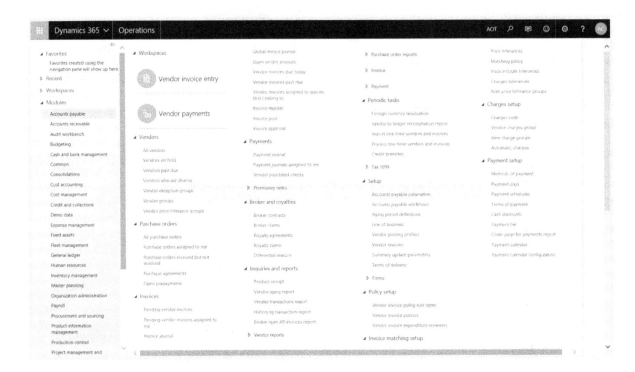

Step 1: Open the All vendors form

To make this change we will need to go to the **All vendors** form.

To do this, open up the navigation panel, expand out the **Modules** group, and click on **Accounts payable** module to see all of the menu items that are available. Then click on the **All vendors** menu item within the **Vendors** menu group.

dync
www.dynamicscompanions.com
Dynamics Companions

- 42 -

www.blindsquirrelpublishing.com
© 2017 Blind Squirrel Publishing, LLC, All Rights Reserved

BLIND SQUIRREL
PUBLISHING

DYNAMICS COMPANIONS
BARE BONES CONFIGURATION GUIDE

CONFIGURING ACCOUNTS PAYABLE WITHIN DYNAMICS 365 FOR OPERATIONS
MODULE 2: CONFIGURING THE ACCOUNTS PAYABLE VENDOR ACCOUNTS

Creating A New Vendor Account

How to do it...

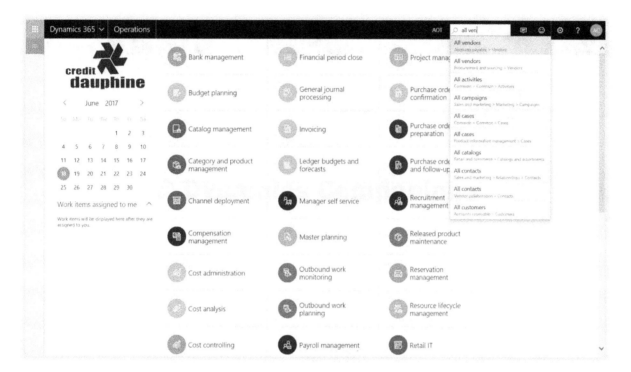

Step 1: Open the All vendors form

Alternatively, you can search for the **All vendors** form by clicking on the search icon in the header of the form (or press **ALT+G)** and then type in **all ven** into the search box. Then you will be able to select the **All vendors** maintenance form from the dropdown list.

dync
www.dynamicscompanions.com
Dynamics Companions

- 43 -

www.blindsquirrelpublishing.com
© 2017 Blind Squirrel Publishing, LLC, All Rights Reserved

BLIND SQUIRREL
PUBLISHING

DYNAMICS COMPANIONS
BARE BONES CONFIGURATION GUIDE

CONFIGURING ACCOUNTS PAYABLE WITHIN DYNAMICS 365 FOR OPERATIONS
MODULE 2: CONFIGURING THE ACCOUNTS PAYABLE VENDOR ACCOUNTS

Creating A New Vendor Account

How to do it...

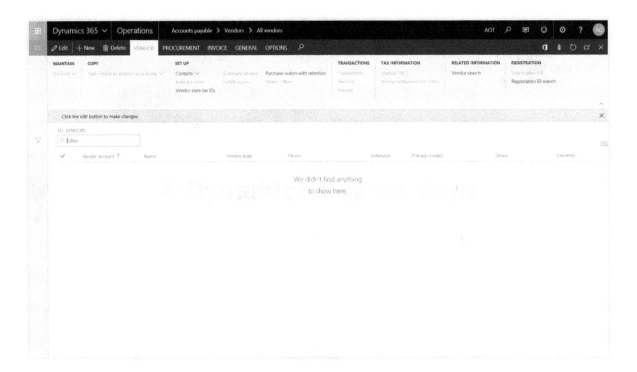

Step 2: Click New

This will open up the **All Vendors** list page where we will access all of the vendors that we have configured in the system.

So now we will want to create our first **Vendor** record.

To do this, just click on the **New** button in the menu bar.

www.dynamicscompanions.com
Dynamics Companions

- 44 -

www.blindsquirrelpublishing.com
© 2017 Blind Squirrel Publishing, LLC, All Rights Reserved

BLIND SQUIRREL
PUBLISHING

DYNAMICS COMPANIONS
BARE BONES CONFIGURATION GUIDE

CONFIGURING ACCOUNTS PAYABLE WITHIN DYNAMICS 365 FOR OPERATIONS
MODULE 2: CONFIGURING THE ACCOUNTS PAYABLE VENDOR ACCOUNTS

Creating A New Vendor Account

How to do it...

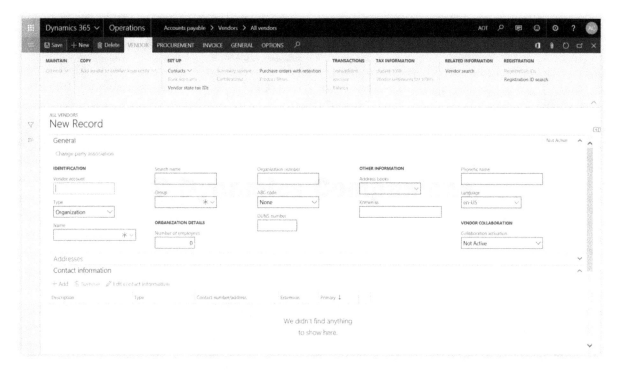

Step 2: Click New

This will open up a new **Vendor** record for us to start to configure.

www.dynamicscompanions.com
Dynamics Companions

- 45 -

www.blindsquirrelpublishing.com
© 2017 Blind Squirrel Publishing, LLC , All Rights Reserved

BLIND SQUIRREL
PUBLISHING

DYNAMICS COMPANIONS
BARE BONES CONFIGURATION GUIDE

CONFIGURING ACCOUNTS PAYABLE WITHIN DYNAMICS 365 FOR OPERATIONS
MODULE 2: CONFIGURING THE ACCOUNTS PAYABLE VENDOR ACCOUNTS

Creating A New Vendor Account

How to do it...

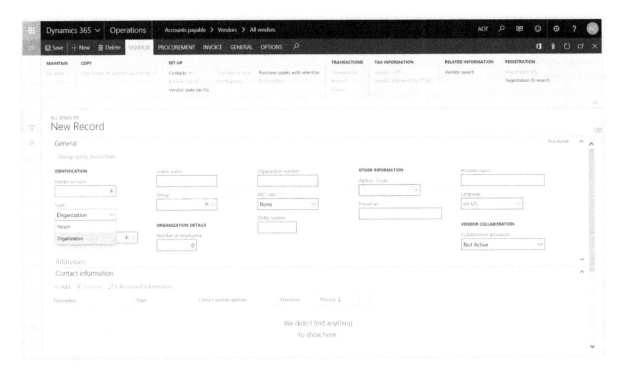

Step 3: Select the Record type

Vendors can either be an individual or an organization within the system.

By default the record type is **Organization** but if we want to create a vendor that is an person then we will want to change the **Record type** of the **Vendor**.

To do this, click on the **Record Type** drop-down list and you will be able to select the type of party that you will associate with the vendor.

If we were creating a **Vendor** record that is an individual, then we would set the **Record type** to **Person.**

www.dynamicscompanions.com
Dynamics Companions

- 46 -

www.blindsquirrelpublishing.com
© 2017 Blind Squirrel Publishing, LLC, All Rights Reserved

BLIND SQUIRREL
PUBLISHING

DYNAMICS COMPANIONS
BARE BONES CONFIGURATION GUIDE

CONFIGURING ACCOUNTS PAYABLE WITHIN DYNAMICS 365 FOR OPERATIONS
MODULE 2: CONFIGURING THE ACCOUNTS PAYABLE VENDOR ACCOUNTS

Creating A New Vendor Account

How to do it...

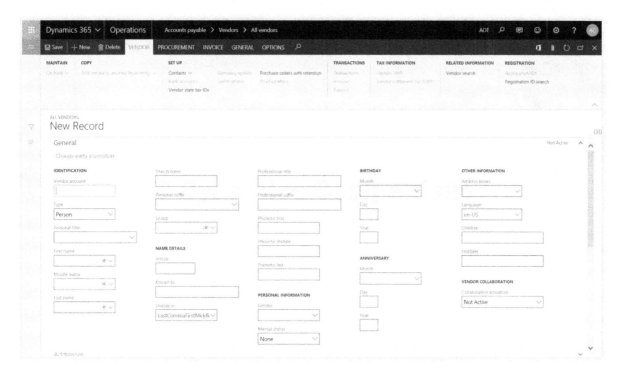

Step 3: Select the Record type

After selecting the **Person** option then we will notice that the naming conventions change to be more person related, allowing us to enter in the **First name**, **Last name** etc.

dync
www.dynamicscompanions.com
Dynamics Companions

- 47 -

www.blindsquirrelpublishing.com
© 2017 Blind Squirrel Publishing, LLC, All Rights Reserved

BLIND SQUIRREL
PUBLISHING

DYNAMICS COMPANIONS
BARE BONES CONFIGURATION GUIDE

CONFIGURING ACCOUNTS PAYABLE WITHIN DYNAMICS 365 FOR OPERATIONS
MODULE 2: CONFIGURING THE ACCOUNTS PAYABLE VENDOR ACCOUNTS

Creating A New Vendor Account

How to do it...

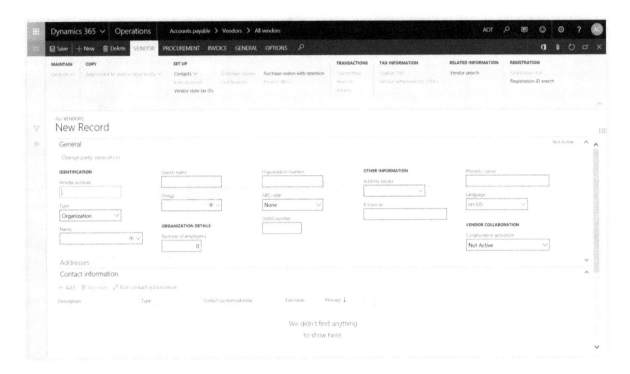

Step 4: Change the Record type to Organization

But If our **Vendor** is a company rather than an individual we will want to have the information that shows be more company specific.

To do this, just click on the **Type** again and select the type of record that you want to use.

For this record we will change the **Record Type** to **Organization**.

After selecting the **Organization** option then we will notice that the naming conventions change to be more company related, allowing us to enter in only the **Name**.

www.dynamicscompanions.com
Dynamics Companions

- 48 -

www.blindsquirrelpublishing.com
© 2017 Blind Squirrel Publishing, LLC, All Rights Reserved

BLIND SQUIRREL
PUBLISHING

DYNAMICS COMPANIONS
BARE BONES CONFIGURATION GUIDE

CONFIGURING ACCOUNTS PAYABLE WITHIN DYNAMICS 365 FOR OPERATIONS
MODULE 2: CONFIGURING THE ACCOUNTS PAYABLE VENDOR ACCOUNTS

Creating A New Vendor Account

How to do it...

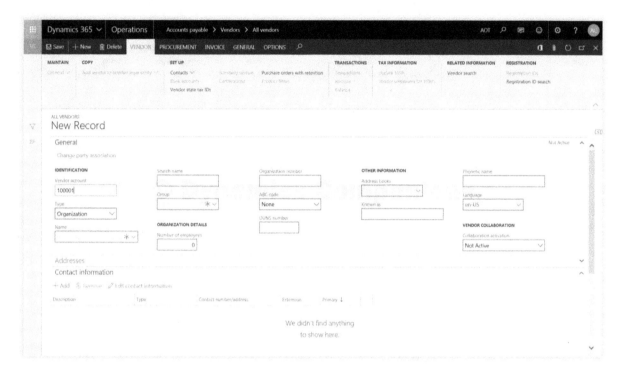

Step 5: Set the Vendor account code

Now that we have selected the type of **Vendor** that we are adding we can continue on to add all of the vendor details.

We will start this off by assigning our **Vendor** a **Vendor account** code.

To do this we will just set the **Vendor account** number that you want to associate with the vendor record.

For the first vendor we will set the **Vendor account** to **100001.**

dyn c
www.dynamicscompanions.com
Dynamics Companions

- 49 -

www.blindsquirrelpublishing.com
© 2017 Blind Squirrel Publishing, LLC , All Rights Reserved

BLIND SQUIRREL
PUBLISHING

DYNAMICS COMPANIONS
BARE BONES CONFIGURATION GUIDE

CONFIGURING ACCOUNTS PAYABLE WITHIN DYNAMICS 365 FOR OPERATIONS
MODULE 2: CONFIGURING THE ACCOUNTS PAYABLE VENDOR ACCOUNTS

Creating A New Vendor Account

How to do it...

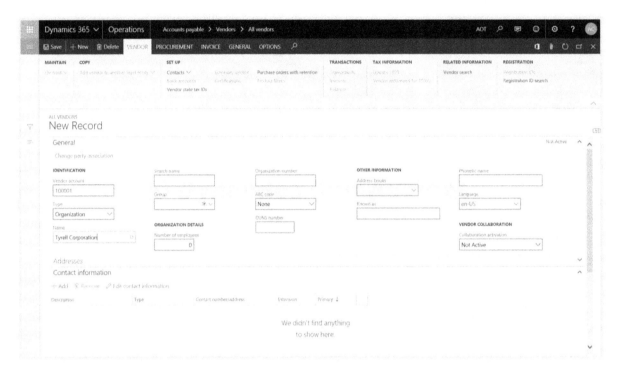

Step 6: Set the vendor Name

Next we will want to give our vendor a **Name** make them easier to search for.

To Then type in the **Name** of the organization.

Here we set the Name to *Tyrell Corporation*.

dync
www.dynamicscompanions.com
Dynamics Companions
- 50 -
www.blindsquirrelpublishing.com
© 2017 Blind Squirrel Publishing, LLC, All Rights Reserved
BLIND SQUIRREL
PUBLISHING

DYNAMICS COMPANIONS
BARE BONES CONFIGURATION GUIDE

CONFIGURING ACCOUNTS PAYABLE WITHIN DYNAMICS 365 FOR OPERATIONS
MODULE 2: CONFIGURING THE ACCOUNTS PAYABLE VENDOR ACCOUNTS

Creating A New Vendor Account

How to do it...

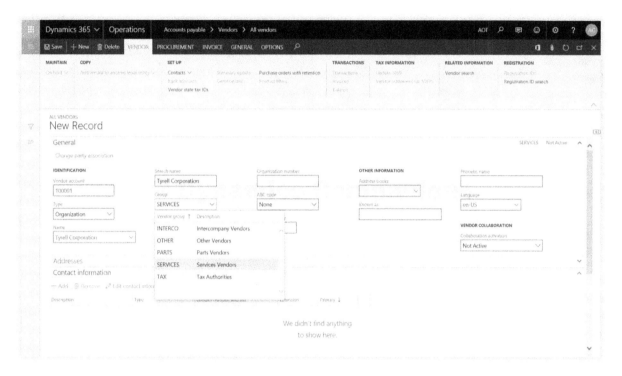

Step 7: Select the vendor Group

Next we will want to assign our **Vendor** to a **Vendor Group**.

This will allow the **Vendor** to inherit the default values that we set up on the **Vendor group** records that we created in the previous step, and save us time from manually configuring some of the codes.

To do this, all we need to do is click on the drop-down list for the **Group** field and select the **Vendor group** that you want to assign to this vendor.

For this vendor, they are a consulting vendor, so we will set the **Group** to *SERVICES*.

www.dynamicscompanions.com
Dynamics Companions

- 51 -

www.blindsquirrelpublishing.com
© 2017 Blind Squirrel Publishing, LLC, All Rights Reserved

BLIND SQUIRREL
PUBLISHING

DYNAMICS COMPANIONS
BARE BONES CONFIGURATION GUIDE

CONFIGURING ACCOUNTS PAYABLE WITHIN DYNAMICS 365 FOR OPERATIONS
MODULE 2: CONFIGURING THE ACCOUNTS PAYABLE VENDOR ACCOUNTS

Creating A New Vendor Account

How to do it...

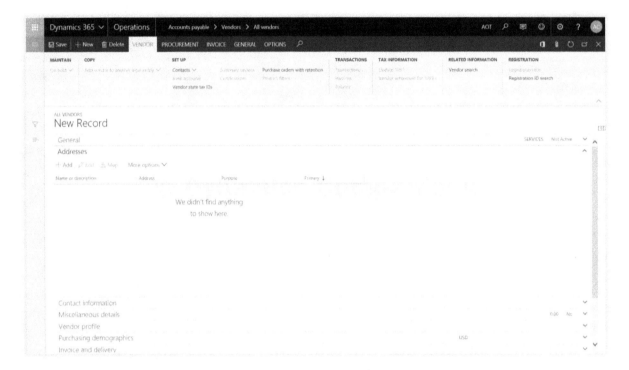

Step 8: Click on the Add button within the Addresses group

Now we will want to set up an address for our vendor.

To do this, expand out the **Addresses** tab group and we will be able to see that there are some functions that will allow us to manage the vendor addresses.

To add a new address we just need to click on the **Add** button within the grids menu bar.

dyn c
dynamics companions

www.dynamicscompanions.com
Dynamics Companions

- 52 -

www.blindsquirrelpublishing.com
© 2017 Blind Squirrel Publishing, LLC, All Rights Reserved

BLIND SQUIRREL
PUBLISHING

DYNAMICS COMPANIONS
BARE BONES CONFIGURATION GUIDE

CONFIGURING ACCOUNTS PAYABLE WITHIN DYNAMICS 365 FOR OPERATIONS
MODULE 2: CONFIGURING THE ACCOUNTS PAYABLE VENDOR ACCOUNTS

Creating A New Vendor Account

How to do it...

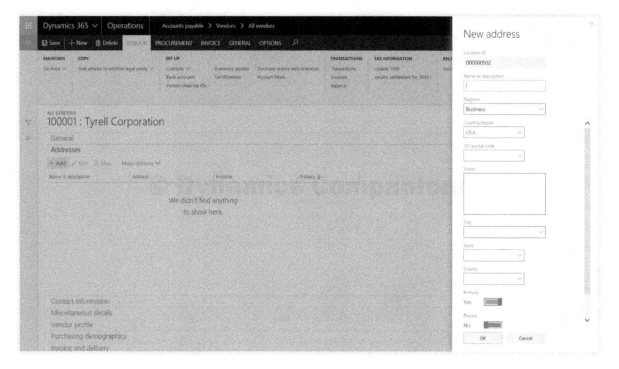

Step 8: Click on the Add button within the Addresses group

This will open up a **New Address** dialog box where we will be able start configuring our new address for the vendor.

www.dynamicscompanions.com
Dynamics Companions

- 53 -

www.blindsquirrelpublishing.com
© 2017 Blind Squirrel Publishing, LLC , All Rights Reserved

BLIND SQUIRREL
PUBLISHING

DYNAMICS COMPANIONS
BARE BONES CONFIGURATION GUIDE

CONFIGURING ACCOUNTS PAYABLE WITHIN DYNAMICS 365 FOR OPERATIONS
MODULE 2: CONFIGURING THE ACCOUNTS PAYABLE VENDOR ACCOUNTS

Creating A New Vendor Account

How to do it...

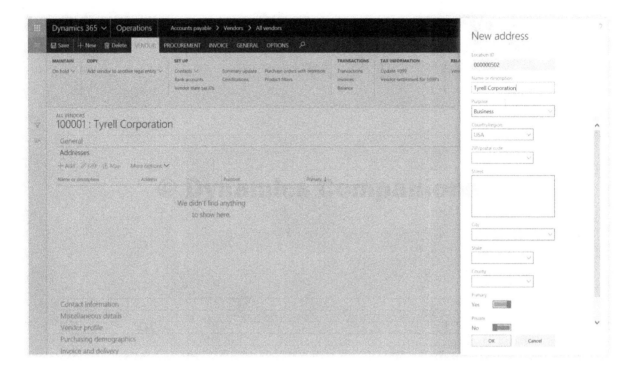

Step 9: Set the Name or description

Now we will want to assign the **Address** name that we can easily locate it with.

To do this we will just type in a **Name or description** for the address.

For this address, since it is the default address for the vendor, we will set the **Name or address** to **Tyrell Corporation** to match the name on the vendor.

dync

www.dynamicscompanions.com
Dynamics Companions

- 54 -

www.blindsquirrelpublishing.com
© 2017 Blind Squirrel Publishing, LLC, All Rights Reserved

BLIND SQUIRREL
PUBLISHING

DYNAMICS COMPANIONS
BARE BONES CONFIGURATION GUIDE

CONFIGURING ACCOUNTS PAYABLE WITHIN DYNAMICS 365 FOR OPERATIONS
MODULE 2: CONFIGURING THE ACCOUNTS PAYABLE VENDOR ACCOUNTS

Creating A New Vendor Account

How to do it...

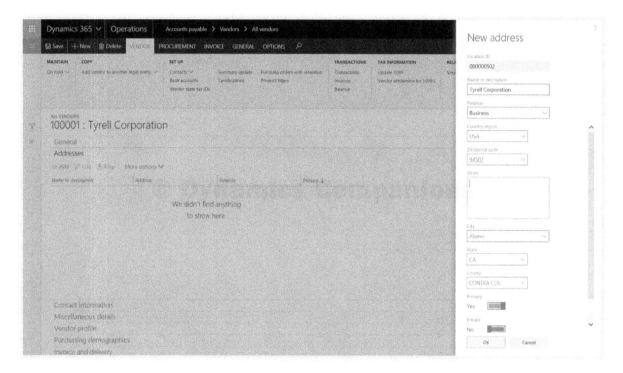

Step 10: Enter in a Zip/postal code

Next we will want to specify the **Zip/Postal code** for the address

To do this, just type in the **Zip/Postal Code** for the address.

For this vendor, we will set the **Zip/Postal code** to **94507**.

Notice that it also fills in all of the **City**, **State** and **County** information for you.

dync
www.dynamicscompanions.com
Dynamics Companions

- 55 -

www.blindsquirrelpublishing.com
© 2017 Blind Squirrel Publishing, LLC, All Rights Reserved

BLIND SQUIRREL
PUBLISHING

DYNAMICS COMPANIONS
BARE BONES CONFIGURATION GUIDE

CONFIGURING ACCOUNTS PAYABLE WITHIN DYNAMICS 365 FOR OPERATIONS
MODULE 2: CONFIGURING THE ACCOUNTS PAYABLE VENDOR ACCOUNTS

Creating A New Vendor Account

How to do it...

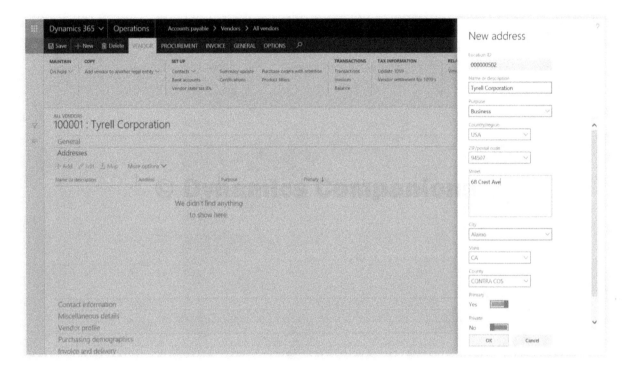

Step 11: Enter in the Street

Next we will want specify the **Street** address for the vendor.

To do this, just enter in the street address into the **Street** field.

For this address we set the **Street** to **68 Crest Ave.**

When we have done that, we can just click on the **OK** button to save the address.

dync
www.dynamicscompanions.com
Dynamics Companions

- 56 -

www.blindsquirrelpublishing.com
© 2017 Blind Squirrel Publishing, LLC, All Rights Reserved

BLIND SQUIRREL
PUBLISHING

DYNAMICS COMPANIONS
BARE BONES CONFIGURATION GUIDE

CONFIGURING ACCOUNTS PAYABLE WITHIN DYNAMICS 365 FOR OPERATIONS
MODULE 2: CONFIGURING THE ACCOUNTS PAYABLE VENDOR ACCOUNTS

Creating A New Vendor Account

How to do it...

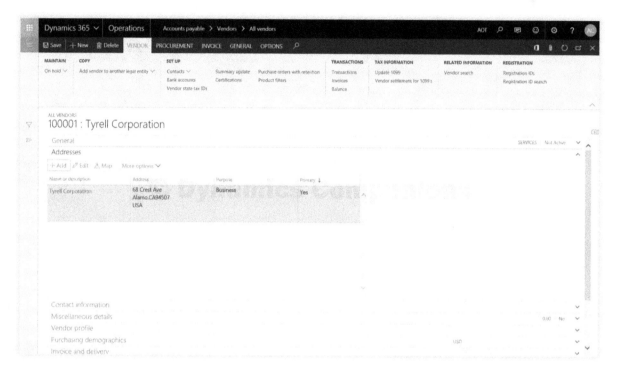

Step 11: Enter in the Street

Now you will see that the address has been added to your vendor account.

www.dynamicscompanions.com
Dynamics Companions

- 57 -

www.blindsquirrelpublishing.com
© 2017 Blind Squirrel Publishing, LLC, All Rights Reserved

BLIND SQUIRREL
PUBLISHING

DYNAMICS COMPANIONS
BARE BONES CONFIGURATION GUIDE

CONFIGURING ACCOUNTS PAYABLE WITHIN DYNAMICS 365 FOR OPERATIONS
MODULE 2: CONFIGURING THE ACCOUNTS PAYABLE VENDOR ACCOUNTS

Creating A New Vendor Account

How to do it...

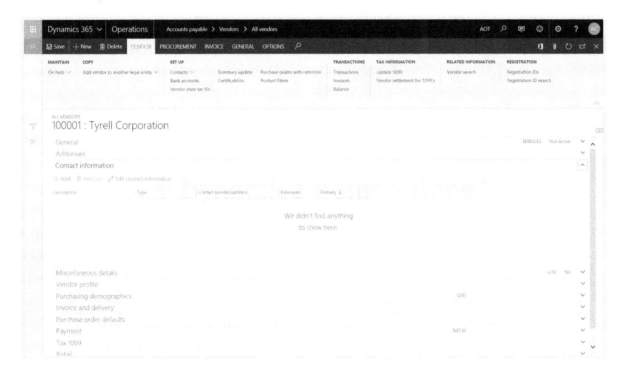

Step 12: Click Add within the Contact information

Now we will want to add some contact information for our vendor.

To do this, just expand out the **Contact Information** tab group and then click on the **+ Add** button within the group.

dyn_c   www.dynamicscompanions.com
Dynamics Companions

- 58 -

www.blindsquirrelpublishing.com
© 2017 Blind Squirrel Publishing, LLC, All Rights Reserved

BLIND SQUIRREL
PUBLISHING

DYNAMICS COMPANIONS
BARE BONES CONFIGURATION GUIDE

CONFIGURING ACCOUNTS PAYABLE WITHIN DYNAMICS 365 FOR OPERATIONS
MODULE 2: CONFIGURING THE ACCOUNTS PAYABLE VENDOR ACCOUNTS

Creating A New Vendor Account

How to do it...

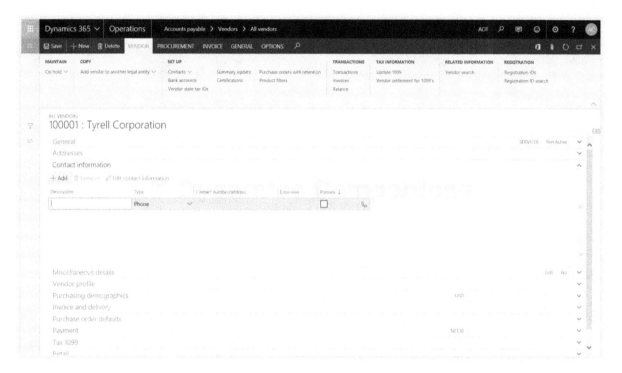

Step 12: Click Add within the Contact information

This will create a new contact record for us within the vendor details.

dync
www.dynamicscompanions.com
Dynamics Companions

- 59 -

www.blindsquirrelpublishing.com
© 2017 Blind Squirrel Publishing, LLC, All Rights Reserved

BLIND SQUIRREL
PUBLISHING

DYNAMICS COMPANIONS
BARE BONES CONFIGURATION GUIDE

CONFIGURING ACCOUNTS PAYABLE WITHIN DYNAMICS 365 FOR OPERATIONS
MODULE 2: CONFIGURING THE ACCOUNTS PAYABLE VENDOR ACCOUNTS

Creating A New Vendor Account

How to do it...

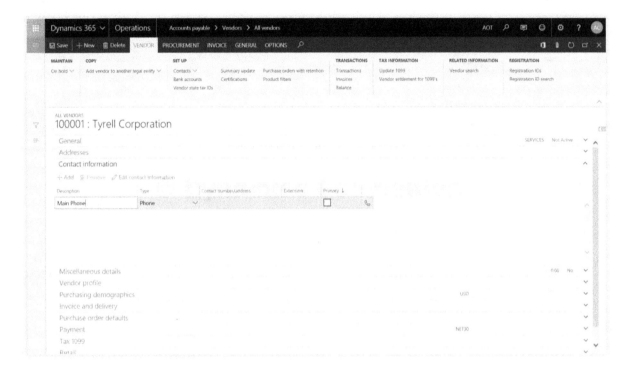

Step 13: Enter a Description

We will want to start by giving our contact record a description to identify it.

To do this, just type in a **Description** for the contact record.

In this example, we set the **Description** to **Main Phone.**

www.dynamicscompanions.com
Dynamics Companions

- 60 -

www.blindsquirrelpublishing.com
© 2017 Blind Squirrel Publishing, LLC, All Rights Reserved

BLIND SQUIRREL
PUBLISHING

DYNAMICS COMPANIONS
BARE BONES CONFIGURATION GUIDE

CONFIGURING ACCOUNTS PAYABLE WITHIN DYNAMICS 365 FOR OPERATIONS
MODULE 2: CONFIGURING THE ACCOUNTS PAYABLE VENDOR ACCOUNTS

Creating A New Vendor Account

How to do it...

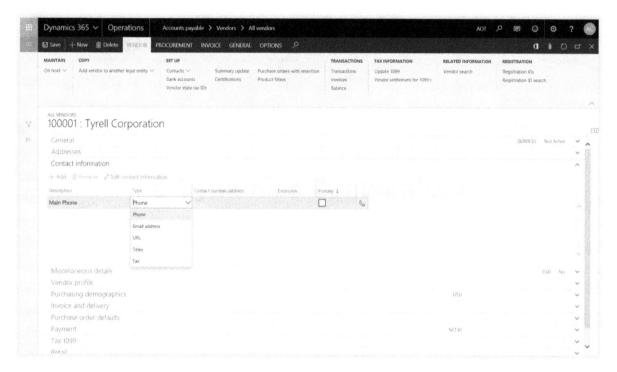

Step 14: Select the contact information Type

Now we will want to specify the type of contact information that this record is associated with – i.e. **Phone**, **e-Mail**, **URL** etc.

To do this, click on the **Type** drop-down list and select the type of contact information you are adding.

For this example, we will click on the **Type** drop-down list and select the **Phone** option.

dync
www.dynamicscompanions.com
Dynamics Companions

- 61 -

www.blindsquirrelpublishing.com
© 2017 Blind Squirrel Publishing, LLC, All Rights Reserved

BLIND SQUIRREL
PUBLISHING

DYNAMICS COMPANIONS
BARE BONES CONFIGURATION GUIDE

CONFIGURING ACCOUNTS PAYABLE WITHIN DYNAMICS 365 FOR OPERATIONS
MODULE 2: CONFIGURING THE ACCOUNTS PAYABLE VENDOR ACCOUNTS

Creating A New Vendor Account

How to do it...

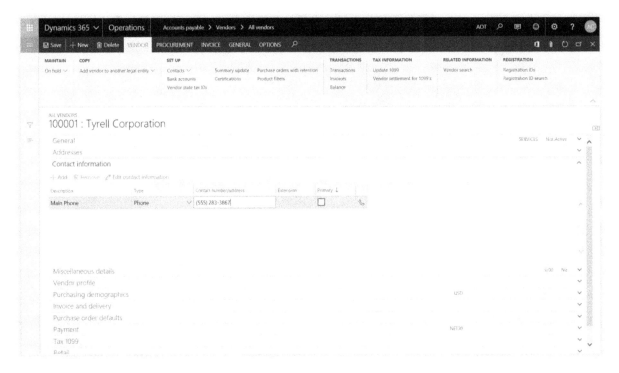

Step 15: Enter in the Contact number/address

Now we will want to enter in the contact number or email address for the contact record.

To do this, just type in the phone number or email address into the **Contact Number/Address** field.

For this example we set the Contact number/address to (555) 283-3867

dyn⊂   www.dynamicscompanions.com
Dynamics Companions

- 62 -

www.blindsquirrelpublishing.com
© 2017 Blind Squirrel Publishing, LLC , All Rights Reserved

BLIND SQUIRREL
PUBLISHING

DYNAMICS COMPANIONS
BARE BONES CONFIGURATION GUIDE

CONFIGURING ACCOUNTS PAYABLE WITHIN DYNAMICS 365 FOR OPERATIONS
MODULE 2: CONFIGURING THE ACCOUNTS PAYABLE VENDOR ACCOUNTS

Creating A New Vendor Account

How to do it...

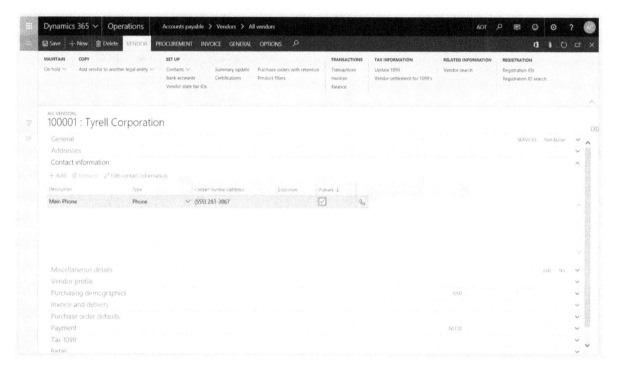

Step 16: Set the Primary flag

Finally, we may want to flag the contact information as the primary contact method for that specific type of contact.

If you want this to be the default for this type of contact then all you need to do is you check the **Primary** flag for the record.

For this example, the main phone is the primary method that we use to contact this vendor so we set the **Primary** flag to **Checked.**

www.dynamicscompanions.com
Dynamics Companions

- 63 -

www.blindsquirrelpublishing.com
© 2017 Blind Squirrel Publishing, LLC, All Rights Reserved

BLIND SQUIRREL
PUBLISHING

DYNAMICS COMPANIONS
BARE BONES CONFIGURATION GUIDE

CONFIGURING ACCOUNTS PAYABLE WITHIN DYNAMICS 365 FOR OPERATIONS
MODULE 2: CONFIGURING THE ACCOUNTS PAYABLE VENDOR ACCOUNTS

Creating A New Vendor Account

How to do it...

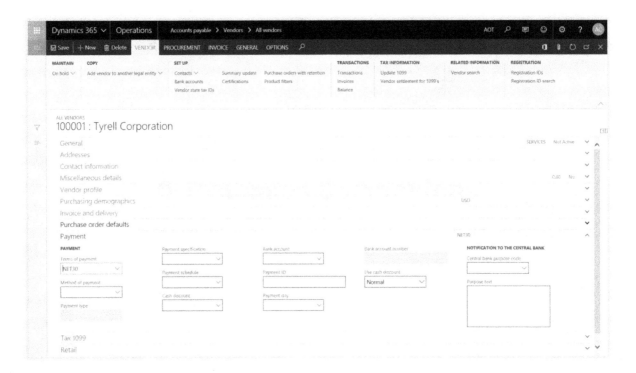

Step 17: Expand the Payments tab group

Now we will want to configure some of the payment defaults for the vendor.

To start doing this, expand the **Payment** tab group.

You will see that there is a lot more information here that you can configure for the vendor, and that some of the information has already been defaulted in off the vendor group.

www.dynamicscompanions.com
Dynamics Companions

- 64 -

www.blindsquirrelpublishing.com
© 2017 Blind Squirrel Publishing, LLC, All Rights Reserved

BLIND SQUIRREL
PUBLISHING

DYNAMICS COMPANIONS
BARE BONES CONFIGURATION GUIDE

CONFIGURING ACCOUNTS PAYABLE WITHIN DYNAMICS 365 FOR OPERATIONS
MODULE 2: CONFIGURING THE ACCOUNTS PAYABLE VENDOR ACCOUNTS

Creating A New Vendor Account

How to do it...

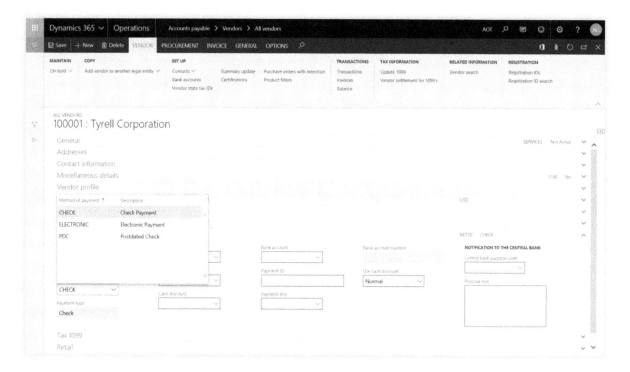

Step 18: Set the default Method of payment

Now we will want to set the default way that we will want to pay the vendor by specifying the **Method of payment.**

To do this, click on the drop-down list for the **Method of Payment** and select the default way that you will pay the vendor.

For this vendor we will want to print a check for them as the default payment method, so we will click on the **Method of payment** drop-down list and then select the **CHECK** option.

dyn c
www.dynamicscompanions.com
Dynamics Companions

- 65 -

www.blindsquirrelpublishing.com
© 2017 Blind Squirrel Publishing, LLC , All Rights Reserved
BLIND SQUIRREL PUBLISHING

DYNAMICS COMPANIONS
BARE BONES CONFIGURATION GUIDE

CONFIGURING ACCOUNTS PAYABLE WITHIN DYNAMICS 365 FOR OPERATIONS
MODULE 2: CONFIGURING THE ACCOUNTS PAYABLE VENDOR ACCOUNTS

Creating A New Vendor Account

How to do it...

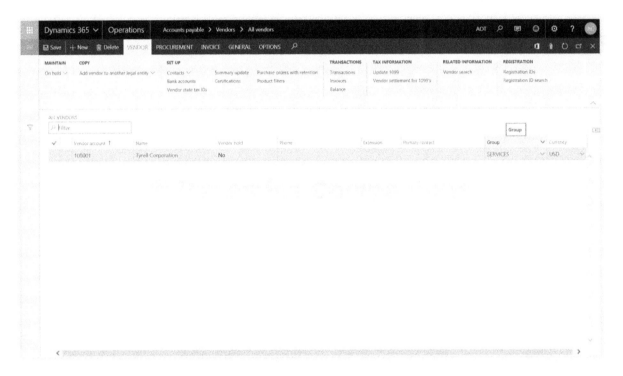

Step 18: Set the default Method of payment

Now when you return back to the **All Vendors** list page you will see that you have a vendor record that you can start using.

dyn c
www.dynamicscompanions.com
Dynamics Companions

- 66 -

www.blindsquirrelpublishing.com
© 2017 Blind Squirrel Publishing, LLC, All Rights Reserved

BLIND SQUIRREL
PUBLISHING

DYNAMICS COMPANIONS
BARE BONES CONFIGURATION GUIDE

CONFIGURING ACCOUNTS PAYABLE WITHIN DYNAMICS 365 FOR OPERATIONS
MODULE 2: CONFIGURING THE ACCOUNTS PAYABLE VENDOR ACCOUNTS

Creating A New Vendor Account

Example Data

Field Name	Value
Vendor account	100001
Record Type	Organization
Name	Tyrell Corporation
Group	SERVICES
Address Zip/Postal Code	94507
Address Street	68 Crest Ave
Contact Description	Main Phone
Contact Type	Phone
Contact Contact number/Address	(555) 283-3867
Contact Primary	Checked
Method of payment	CHECK

Vendor: 100001 – Tyrell Corporation

dync
www.dynamicscompanions.com
Dynamics Companions

- 67 -

www.blindsquirrelpublishing.com
© 2017 Blind Squirrel Publishing, LLC, All Rights Reserved

BLIND SQUIRREL
PUBLISHING

DYNAMICS COMPANIONS
BARE BONES CONFIGURATION GUIDE

CONFIGURING ACCOUNTS PAYABLE WITHIN DYNAMICS 365 FOR OPERATIONS
MODULE 2: CONFIGURING THE ACCOUNTS PAYABLE VENDOR ACCOUNTS

Creating A New Vendor Account

Review

How easy was that? Although there are a lot of different fields that we can configure on the vendor record, we really don't need to populate many of them in order to create our new **Vendors.**

DYNAMICS COMPANIONS
BARE BONES CONFIGURATION GUIDE

CONFIGURING ACCOUNTS PAYABLE WITHIN DYNAMICS 365 FOR OPERATIONS
MODULE 2: CONFIGURING THE ACCOUNTS PAYABLE VENDOR ACCOUNTS

Importing Vendors Using the Excel Workbook Designer

Adding vendors one at a time is good, but if you have a lot of vendors that you want to load into Dynamics AX then you may want to use the **Excel Workbook Designer** to load them all in from a CSV file.

How to do it...

Step 1: Open the Excel workbook designer form

To create our Excel templates we will need to go to the **Excel workbook designer** form.

Navigate to Organization administration > Setup > Office Integration > Excel workbook designer

Step 2: Choose entity, select Field and click ->

The first thing that we need to do here is to find the **Entity** that we want to create the import worksheet for.

Select the **Vendor** entity, click on the **Vendor account** field and then click on the **->** button.

Step 3: Repeat and select the rest of the fields

Now we will add the rest of the fields that we want in the template.

Find the **VendorPartyType** field and move it to the **Selected fields** list.

Find the **Name** field and move it to the **Selected fields** list.

Find the **Street** field and move it to the **Selected fields** list.

Find the **City** field and move it to the **Selected fields** list.

Find the **State** field and move it to the **Selected fields** list.

Find the **Zip/postal code** field and move it to the **Selected fields** list.

Find the **Currency** field and move it to the **Selected fields** list.

Find the **Currency** field and move it to the **Selected fields** list.

Find the **Group** field and move it to the **Selected fields** list.

Step 4: Click Create workbook

Now that we have selected all of the fields that we need for the import we will want to create the template workbook.

Click on the **Create workbook** button in the menu bar.

For this example, we will want to work with the file locally.

Click on the **Download** button.

Now we will want to open up a local copy of the workbook.

Click on the **Open** button

Step 5: Click Enable editing

The workbook will be in read only mode initially.

Click on the **Enable editing** button

dync
www.dynamicscompanions.com
Dynamics Companions

- 69 -

www.blindsquirrelpublishing.com
© 2017 Blind Squirrel Publishing, LLC, All Rights Reserved

BLIND SQUIRREL
PUBLISHING

DYNAMICS COMPANIONS
BARE BONES CONFIGURATION GUIDE

CONFIGURING ACCOUNTS PAYABLE WITHIN DYNAMICS 365 FOR OPERATIONS
MODULE 2: CONFIGURING THE ACCOUNTS PAYABLE VENDOR ACCOUNTS

Importing Vendors Using the Excel Workbook Designer

How to do it...

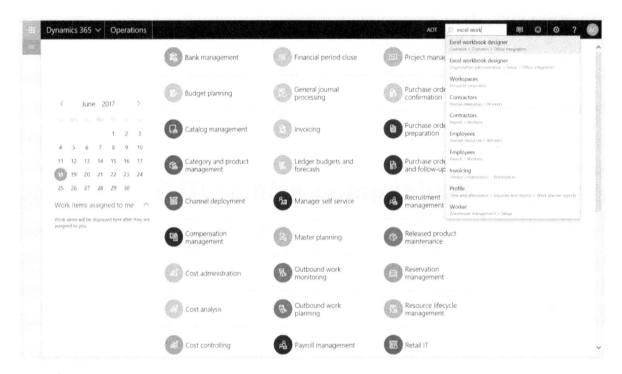

Step 1: Open the Excel workbook designer form

To create our Excel templates we will need to go to the **Excel workbook designer** form.

To do this, open up the navigation panel, expand out the **Modules** group, and click on the **Organization administration** module to see all of the menu items that are available. Then click on the **Excel workbook designer** menu item within the **Office integration** subgroup of the **Setup** menu group.

Alternatively, you can search for **Excel workbook designer** form by clicking on the search icon in the header of the form (or press **ALT+G**) and then type in **excel work** into the search box. Then you will be able to select the **Excel workbook designer** maintenance form from the dropdown list.

dyn c
www.dynamicscompanions.com
Dynamics Companions

- 70 -

www.blindsquirrelpublishing.com
© 2017 Blind Squirrel Publishing, LLC, All Rights Reserved

BLIND SQUIRREL
PUBLISHING

DYNAMICS COMPANIONS
BARE BONES CONFIGURATION GUIDE

CONFIGURING ACCOUNTS PAYABLE WITHIN DYNAMICS 365 FOR OPERATIONS
MODULE 2: CONFIGURING THE ACCOUNTS PAYABLE VENDOR ACCOUNTS

Importing Vendors Using the Excel Workbook Designer

How to do it...

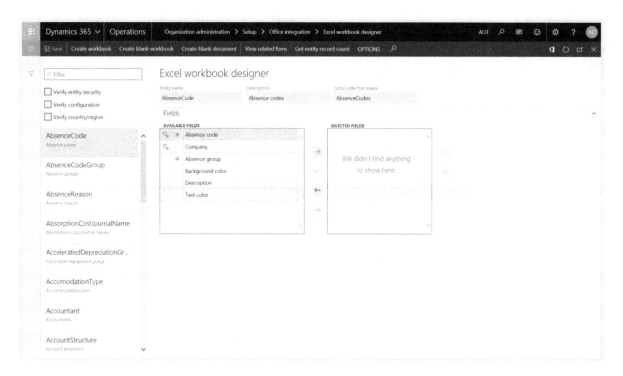

Step 1: Open the Excel workbook designer form

This will open up the **Excel workbook designer** form which allows us to create Excel workbooks that are linked back to the data within Dynamics 365 and then access and publish records.

dyn

www.dynamicscompanions.com
Dynamics Companions

- 71 -

www.blindsquirrelpublishing.com
© 2017 Blind Squirrel Publishing, LLC, All Rights Reserved

BLIND SQUIRREL
PUBLISHING

DYNAMICS COMPANIONS
BARE BONES CONFIGURATION GUIDE

CONFIGURING ACCOUNTS PAYABLE WITHIN DYNAMICS 365 FOR OPERATIONS
MODULE 2: CONFIGURING THE ACCOUNTS PAYABLE VENDOR ACCOUNTS

Importing Vendors Using the Excel Workbook Designer

How to do it...

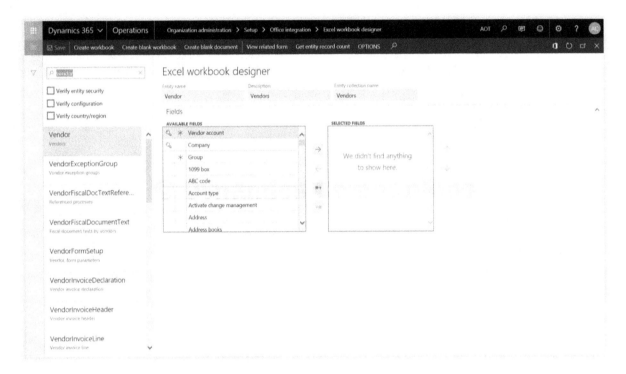

Step 2: Choose entity, select Field and click ->

The first thing that we need to do here is to find the **Entity** that we want to create the import worksheet for.

To do this just select the **Entity,** select a field and then click on the **->** button.

In this case we will want to create the import template for the **Vendor** entity, so we can either scroll through all of the entities until we find it, or type in **Vendor** into the search box and filter out the entities until we can see the **Vendor** entity and then select it.

In the **Available fields** section we will see all of the fields that we can add to our template and in the **Selected fields** section are all of the fields that we have selected. All we need to do is select the fields from the left and add them to the right hand side.

Start off by selecting the **Vendor account** field and then click on the **->** button.

dync
www.dynamicscompanions.com
Dynamics Companions

- 72 -

www.blindsquirrelpublishing.com
© 2017 Blind Squirrel Publishing, LLC, All Rights Reserved

BLIND SQUIRREL
PUBLISHING

DYNAMICS COMPANIONS
BARE BONES CONFIGURATION GUIDE

CONFIGURING ACCOUNTS PAYABLE WITHIN DYNAMICS 365 FOR OPERATIONS
MODULE 2: CONFIGURING THE ACCOUNTS PAYABLE VENDOR ACCOUNTS

Importing Vendors Using the Excel Workbook Designer

How to do it...

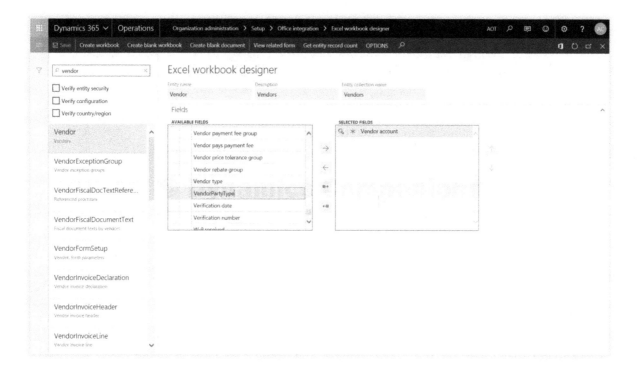

Step 3: Repeat and select the rest of the fields

That will move the **Vendor account** over to the selected fields.

Now we will add the rest of the fields that we want in the template.

To do this, just scroll down to find the next field and then click on the **->** button.

For the next field we will scroll down a little in the list and find the **VendorPartyType** field and move it to the **Selected fields** list.

dynɔ
www.dynamicscompanions.com
Dynamics Companions

- 73 -

www.blindsquirrelpublishing.com
© 2017 Blind Squirrel Publishing, LLC, All Rights Reserved

BLIND SQUIRREL
PUBLISHING

DYNAMICS COMPANIONS
BARE BONES CONFIGURATION GUIDE

CONFIGURING ACCOUNTS PAYABLE WITHIN DYNAMICS 365 FOR OPERATIONS
MODULE 2: CONFIGURING THE ACCOUNTS PAYABLE VENDOR ACCOUNTS

Importing Vendors Using the Excel Workbook Designer

How to do it...

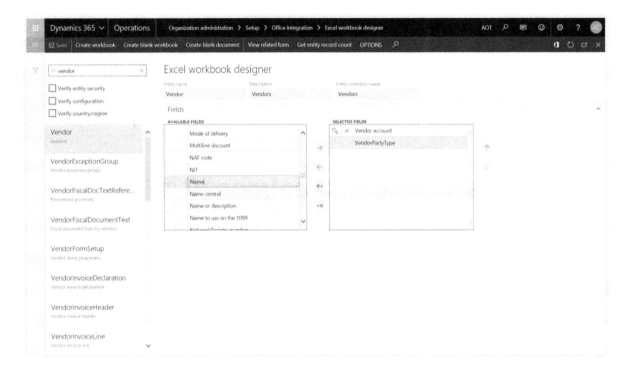

Step 3: Repeat and select the rest of the fields

Now find the **Name** field and move it to the **Selected fields** list.

www.dynamicscompanions.com
Dynamics Companions

- 74 -

www.blindsquirrelpublishing.com
© 2017 Blind Squirrel Publishing, LLC, All Rights Reserved

BLIND SQUIRREL
PUBLISHING

DYNAMICS COMPANIONS
BARE BONES CONFIGURATION GUIDE

CONFIGURING ACCOUNTS PAYABLE WITHIN DYNAMICS 365 FOR OPERATIONS
MODULE 2: CONFIGURING THE ACCOUNTS PAYABLE VENDOR ACCOUNTS

Importing Vendors Using the Excel Workbook Designer

How to do it...

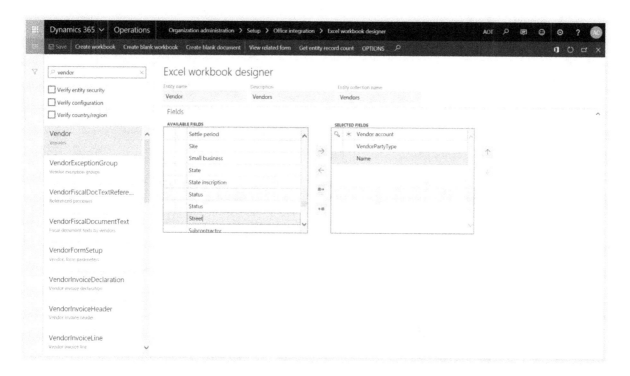

Step 3: Repeat and select the rest of the fields

Now find the **Street** field and move it to the **Selected fields** list.

www.dynamicscompanions.com
Dynamics Companions

- 75 -

www.blindsquirrelpublishing.com
© 2017 Blind Squirrel Publishing, LLC, All Rights Reserved

BLIND SQUIRREL
PUBLISHING

DYNAMICS COMPANIONS
BARE BONES CONFIGURATION GUIDE

CONFIGURING ACCOUNTS PAYABLE WITHIN DYNAMICS 365 FOR OPERATIONS
MODULE 2: CONFIGURING THE ACCOUNTS PAYABLE VENDOR ACCOUNTS

Importing Vendors Using the Excel Workbook Designer

How to do it...

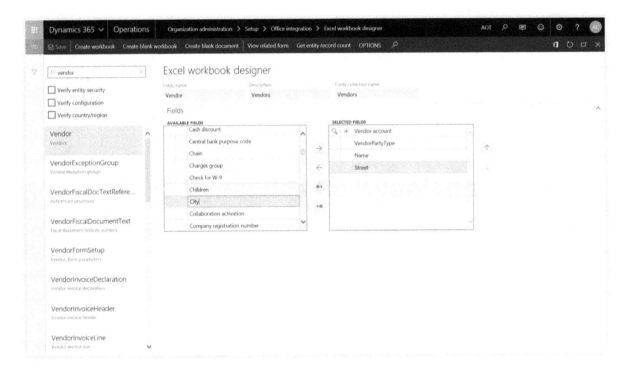

Step 3: Repeat and select the rest of the fields

Now find the **City** field and move it to the **Selected fields** list.

www.dynamicscompanions.com
Dynamics Companions

- 76 -

www.blindsquirrelpublishing.com
© 2017 Blind Squirrel Publishing, LLC, All Rights Reserved

BLIND SQUIRREL
PUBLISHING

DYNAMICS COMPANIONS
BARE BONES CONFIGURATION GUIDE

CONFIGURING ACCOUNTS PAYABLE WITHIN DYNAMICS 365 FOR OPERATIONS
MODULE 2: CONFIGURING THE ACCOUNTS PAYABLE VENDOR ACCOUNTS

Importing Vendors Using the Excel Workbook Designer

How to do it...

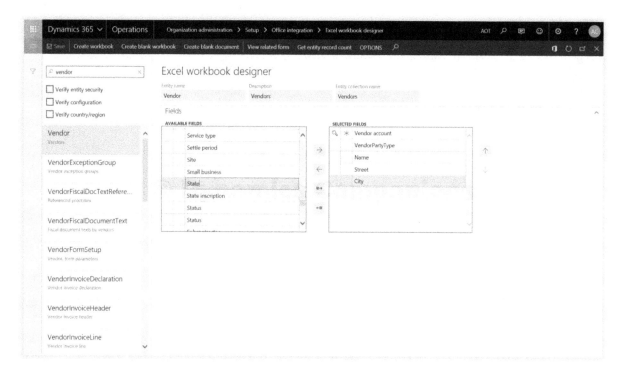

Step 3: Repeat and select the rest of the fields

Now find the **State** field and move it to the **Selected fields** list.

dyn c
www.dynamicscompanions.com
Dynamics Companions

- 77 -

www.blindsquirrelpublishing.com
© 2017 Blind Squirrel Publishing, LLC, All Rights Reserved

BLIND SQUIRREL
PUBLISHING

DYNAMICS COMPANIONS
BARE BONES CONFIGURATION GUIDE

CONFIGURING ACCOUNTS PAYABLE WITHIN DYNAMICS 365 FOR OPERATIONS
MODULE 2: CONFIGURING THE ACCOUNTS PAYABLE VENDOR ACCOUNTS

Importing Vendors Using the Excel Workbook Designer

How to do it...

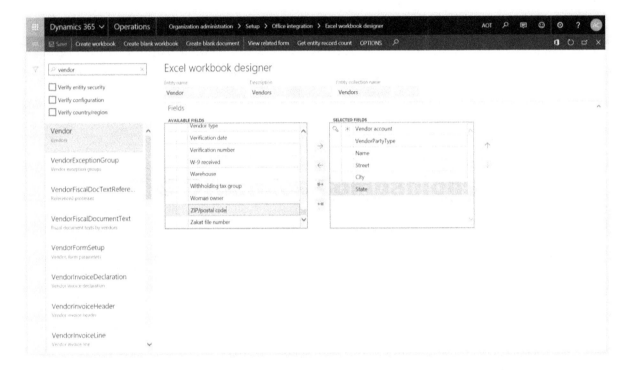

Step 3: Repeat and select the rest of the fields

Now find the **Zip/postal code** field and move it to the **Selected fields** list.

dync
www.dynamicscompanions.com
Dynamics Companions

- 78 -

www.blindsquirrelpublishing.com
© 2017 Blind Squirrel Publishing, LLC, All Rights Reserved

BLIND SQUIRREL
PUBLISHING

DYNAMICS COMPANIONS
BARE BONES CONFIGURATION GUIDE

CONFIGURING ACCOUNTS PAYABLE WITHIN DYNAMICS 365 FOR OPERATIONS
MODULE 2: CONFIGURING THE ACCOUNTS PAYABLE VENDOR ACCOUNTS

Importing Vendors Using the Excel Workbook Designer

How to do it...

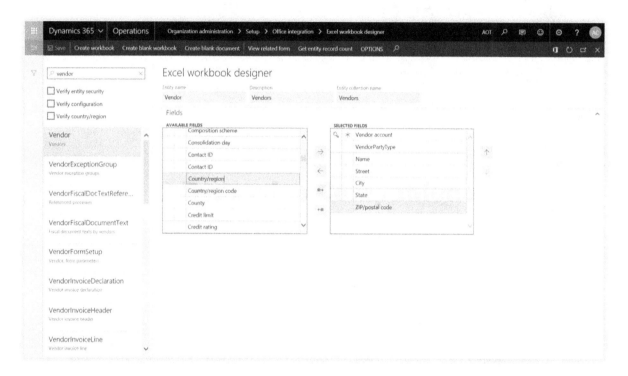

Step 3: Repeat and select the rest of the fields

Now find the **Country/region** field and move it to the **Selected fields** list.

www.dynamicscompanions.com
Dynamics Companions

- 79 -

www.blindsquirrelpublishing.com
© 2017 Blind Squirrel Publishing, LLC, All Rights Reserved

BLIND SQUIRREL
PUBLISHING

DYNAMICS COMPANIONS
BARE BONES CONFIGURATION GUIDE

CONFIGURING ACCOUNTS PAYABLE WITHIN DYNAMICS 365 FOR OPERATIONS
MODULE 2: CONFIGURING THE ACCOUNTS PAYABLE VENDOR ACCOUNTS

Importing Vendors Using the Excel Workbook Designer

How to do it...

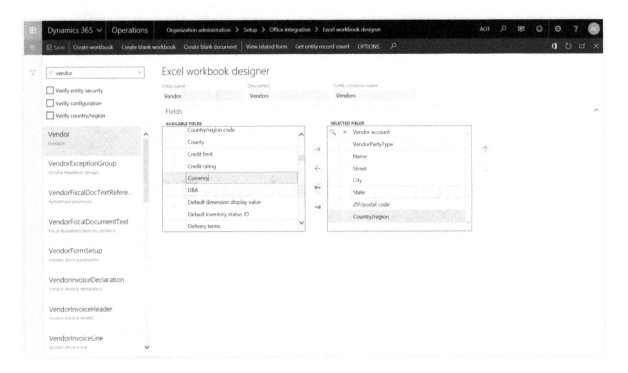

Step 3: Repeat and select the rest of the fields

Now find the **Currency** field and move it to the **Selected fields** list.

www.dynamicscompanions.com
Dynamics Companions

- 80 -

www.blindsquirrelpublishing.com
© 2017 Blind Squirrel Publishing, LLC, All Rights Reserved

BLIND SQUIRREL
PUBLISHING

DYNAMICS COMPANIONS
BARE BONES CONFIGURATION GUIDE

CONFIGURING ACCOUNTS PAYABLE WITHIN DYNAMICS 365 FOR OPERATIONS
MODULE 2: CONFIGURING THE ACCOUNTS PAYABLE VENDOR ACCOUNTS

Importing Vendors Using the Excel Workbook Designer

How to do it...

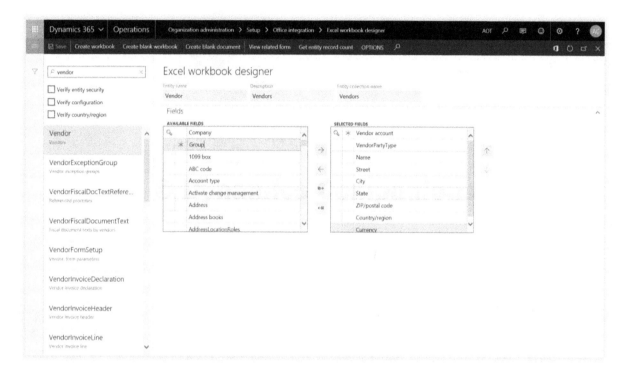

Step 3: Repeat and select the rest of the fields

Now find the **Group** field and move it to the **Selected fields** list.

www.dynamicscompanions.com
Dynamics Companions

- 81 -

www.blindsquirrelpublishing.com
© 2017 Blind Squirrel Publishing, LLC, All Rights Reserved

BLIND SQUIRREL
PUBLISHING

DYNAMICS COMPANIONS
BARE BONES CONFIGURATION GUIDE

CONFIGURING ACCOUNTS PAYABLE WITHIN DYNAMICS 365 FOR OPERATIONS
MODULE 2: CONFIGURIING THE ACCOUNTS PAYABLE VENDOR ACCOUNTS

Importing Vendors Using the Excel Workbook Designer

How to do it...

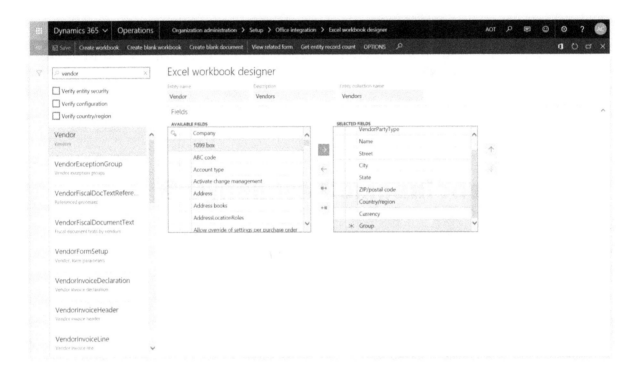

Step 4: Click Create workbook

Now that we have selected all of the fields that we need for the import we will want to create the template workbook.

To do this, just click on the **Create workbook** button in the menu bar.

dync
www.dynamicscompanions.com
Dynamics Companions

- 82 -

www.blindsquirrelpublishing.com
© 2017 Blind Squirrel Publishing, LLC, All Rights Reserved

BLIND SQUIRREL
PUBLISHING

DYNAMICS COMPANIONS
BARE BONES CONFIGURATION GUIDE

CONFIGURING ACCOUNTS PAYABLE WITHIN DYNAMICS 365 FOR OPERATIONS
MODULE 2: CONFIGURING THE ACCOUNTS PAYABLE VENDOR ACCOUNTS

Importing Vendors Using the Excel Workbook Designer

How to do it...

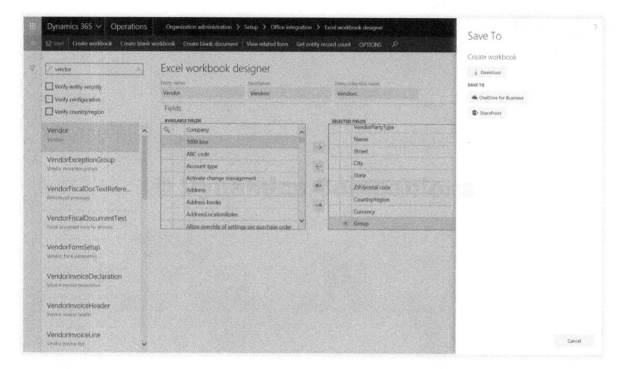

Step 4: Click Create workbook

This will open up a **Save to** dialog box and we just need to choose where we want to save the file to.

For this example, we will want to work with the file locally.

To do this, we will just click on the **Download** button.

www.dynamicscompanions.com
Dynamics Companions

- 83 -

www.blindsquirrelpublishing.com
© 2017 Blind Squirrel Publishing, LLC, All Rights Reserved

BLIND SQUIRREL
PUBLISHING

DYNAMICS COMPANIONS
BARE BONES CONFIGURATION GUIDE

CONFIGURING ACCOUNTS PAYABLE WITHIN DYNAMICS 365 FOR OPERATIONS
MODULE 2: CONFIGURING THE ACCOUNTS PAYABLE VENDOR ACCOUNTS

Importing Vendors Using the Excel Workbook Designer

How to do it...

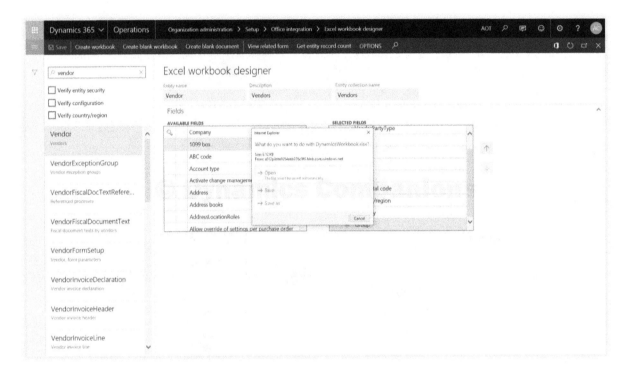

Step 4: Click Create workbook

Then the explorer dialog will be displayed.

Now we will want to open up a local copy of the workbook.

To do this just click on the **Open** button.

DYNAMICS COMPANIONS
BARE BONES CONFIGURATION GUIDE

CONFIGURING ACCOUNTS PAYABLE WITHIN DYNAMICS 365 FOR OPERATIONS
MODULE 2: CONFIGURING THE ACCOUNTS PAYABLE VENDOR ACCOUNTS

Importing Vendors Using the Excel Workbook Designer

How to do it...

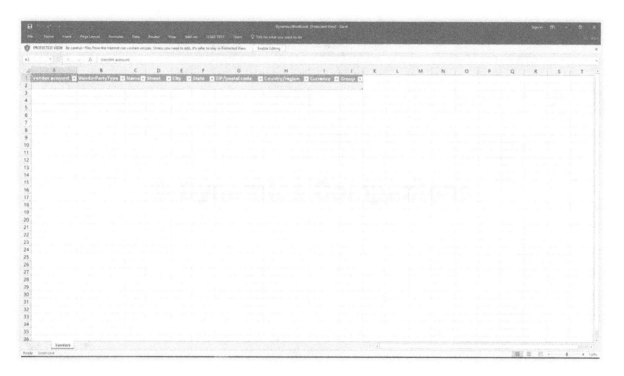

Step 5: Click Enable editing

Next thing you know, Excel will open up and we will see all of the fields that we selected from the entity are showing up as columns.

The workbook will be in read only mode initially.

To activate the worksheet, we just need to click on the **Enable editing** button in the message bar.

dyn c
www.dynamicscompanions.com
Dynamics Companions

- 85 -

www.blindsquirrelpublishing.com
© 2017 Blind Squirrel Publishing, LLC, All Rights Reserved

BLIND SQUIRREL
PUBLISHING

DYNAMICS COMPANIONS
BARE BONES CONFIGURATION GUIDE

CONFIGURING ACCOUNTS PAYABLE WITHIN DYNAMICS 365 FOR OPERATIONS
MODULE 2: CONFIGURING THE ACCOUNTS PAYABLE VENDOR ACCOUNTS

Importing Vendors Using the Excel Workbook Designer

How to do it...

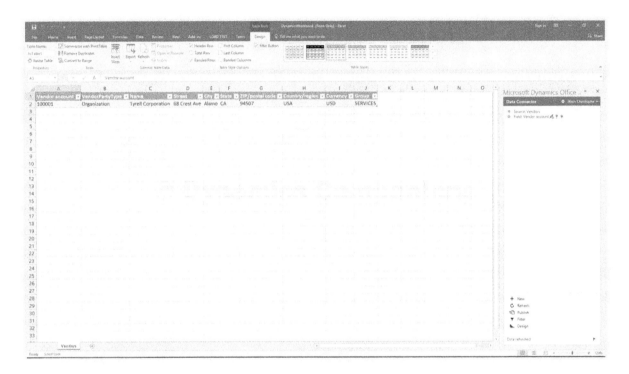

Step 5: Click Enable editing

This will open up a new Excel panel for the integration to Dynamics 365, and also populate the worksheet with all of the existing data. There isn't much right now, but in the next section we will fix that.

dyn c
www.dynamicscompanions.com
Dynamics Companions

- 86 -

www.blindsquirrelpublishing.com
© 2017 Blind Squirrel Publishing, LLC , All Rights Reserved

BLIND SQUIRREL
PUBLISHING

DYNAMICS COMPANIONS
BARE BONES CONFIGURATION GUIDE

CONFIGURING ACCOUNTS PAYABLE WITHIN DYNAMICS 365 FOR OPERATIONS
MODULE 2: CONFIGURING THE ACCOUNTS PAYABLE VENDOR ACCOUNTS

Importing Vendors Using the Excel Workbook Designer

Review

How east is that? The Excel workbook designer is a great tool because it allows you to create your own data import templates through a tool that everyone is familiar with using – Excel.

www.dynamicscompanions.com
Dynamics Companions

- 87 -

www.blindsquirrelpublishing.com
© 2017 Blind Squirrel Publishing, LLC, All Rights Reserved

BLIND SQUIRREL
PUBLISHING

DYNAMICS COMPANIONS
BARE BONES CONFIGURATION GUIDE

CONFIGURING ACCOUNTS PAYABLE WITHIN DYNAMICS 365 FOR OPERATIONS
MODULE 2: CONFIGURING THE ACCOUNTS PAYABLE VENDOR ACCOUNTS

Populating and publishing the Import Template

Now that we have an Excel template we can start taking advantage of it to import in all of our other vendor records.

How to do it...

Step 1: Return to the Excel workbook

Return to the Excel workbook

Step 2: Paste in data and click Publish

Now we can add in all of our other vendor records into the workbook.

Paste in the vendor records and click **Publish**

DYNAMICS COMPANIONS
BARE BONES CONFIGURATION GUIDE

CONFIGURING ACCOUNTS PAYABLE WITHIN DYNAMICS 365 FOR OPERATIONS
MODULE 2: CONFIGURING THE ACCOUNTS PAYABLE VENDOR ACCOUNTS

Populating and publishing the Import Template

How to do it...

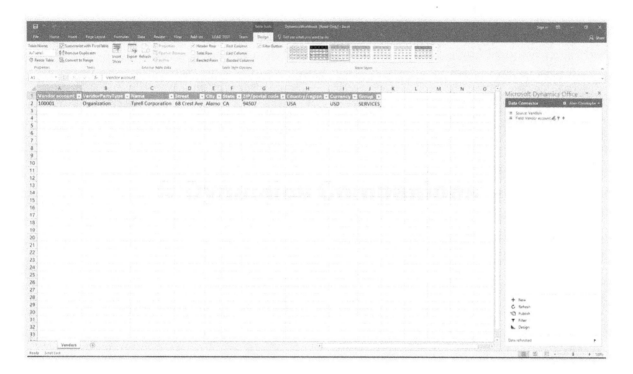

Step 1: Return to the Excel workbook

To do this, return back to the workbook that you just created.

dyn c
dynamics companions

www.dynamicscompanions.com
Dynamics Companions

- 89 -

www.blindsquirrelpublishing.com
© 2017 Blind Squirrel Publishing, LLC , All Rights Reserved

BLIND SQUIRREL
PUBLISHING

DYNAMICS COMPANIONS
BARE BONES CONFIGURATION GUIDE

CONFIGURING ACCOUNTS PAYABLE WITHIN DYNAMICS 365 FOR OPERATIONS
MODULE 2: CONFIGURING THE ACCOUNTS PAYABLE VENDOR ACCOUNTS

Populating and publishing the Import Template

How to do it...

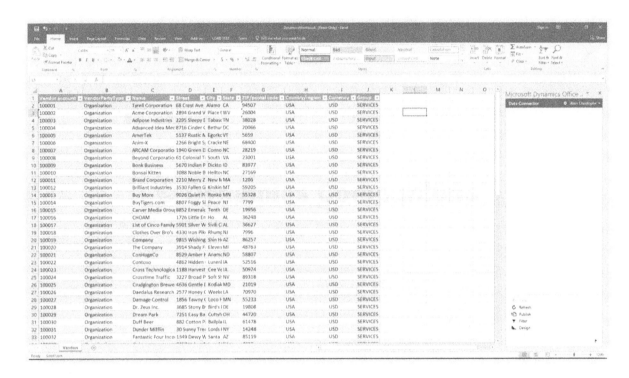

Step 2: Paste in data and click Publish

Now we can add in all of our other vendor records into the workbook.

To do this, just paste in all of the other vendor records that you want to add to Dynamics 365.

Make sure you pay attention to the columns and make sure that all of the address details line up to the right field.

When you are ready to update the system, just click on the **Publish** button within the Add-In panel.

dyn c
www.dynamicscompanions.com
Dynamics Companions

- 90 -

www.blindsquirrelpublishing.com
© 2017 Blind Squirrel Publishing, LLC, All Rights Reserved

BLIND SQUIRREL
PUBLISHING

DYNAMICS COMPANIONS
BARE BONES CONFIGURATION GUIDE

CONFIGURING ACCOUNTS PAYABLE WITHIN DYNAMICS 365 FOR OPERATIONS
MODULE 2: CONFIGURING THE ACCOUNTS PAYABLE VENDOR ACCOUNTS

Populating and publishing the Import Template

How to do it...

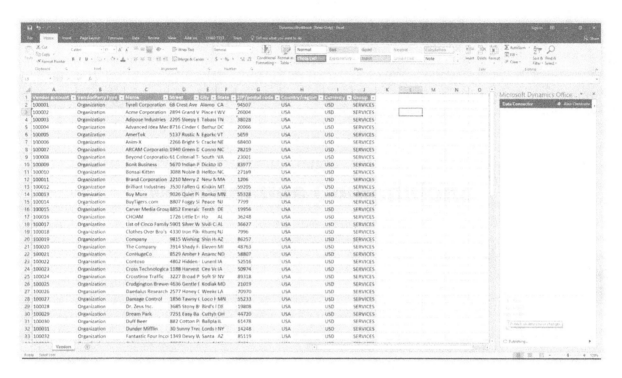

Step 2: Paste in data and click Publish

The panel message at the bottom will change to indicate that the records are publishing.

www.dynamicscompanions.com
Dynamics Companions

- 91 -

www.blindsquirrelpublishing.com
© 2017 Blind Squirrel Publishing, LLC, All Rights Reserved

BLIND SQUIRREL
PUBLISHING

DYNAMICS COMPANIONS
BARE BONES CONFIGURATION GUIDE

CONFIGURING ACCOUNTS PAYABLE WITHIN DYNAMICS 365 FOR OPERATIONS
MODULE 2: CONFIGURING THE ACCOUNTS PAYABLE VENDOR ACCOUNTS

Populating and publishing the Import Template

How to do it...

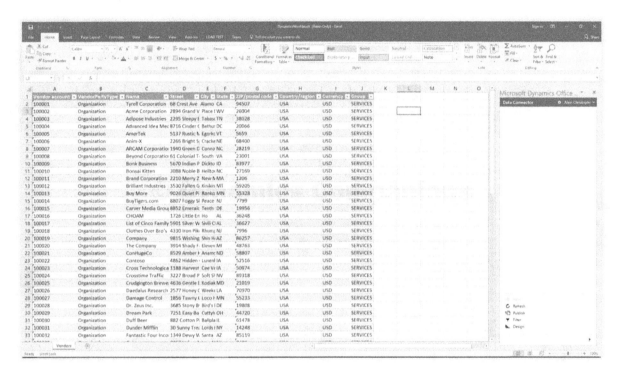

Step 2: Paste in data and click Publish

And after a little bit it will return back and if all of your data is correct, you will see the data refresh and show all of the records.

www.blindsquirrelpublishing.com
© 2017 Blind Squirrel Publishing, LLC, All Rights Reserved

DYNAMICS COMPANIONS
BARE BONES CONFIGURATION GUIDE

CONFIGURING ACCOUNTS PAYABLE WITHIN DYNAMICS 365 FOR OPERATIONS
MODULE 2: CONFIGURING THE ACCOUNTS PAYABLE VENDOR ACCOUNTS

Populating and publishing the Import Template

How to do it...

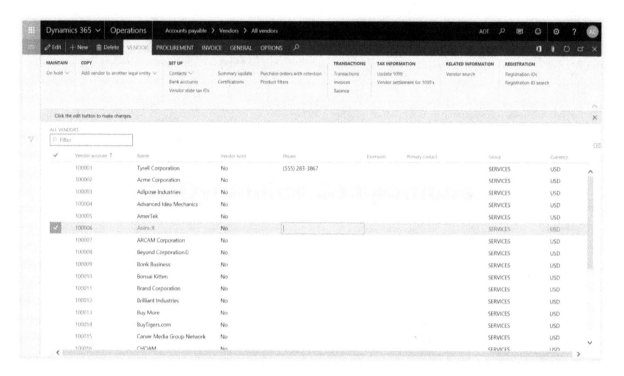

Step 2: Paste in data and click Publish

If you don't trust it, then just open up the **All vendors** form and you will see that all of your new customers have been added to the system.

dyn c
dynamics companions

www.dynamicscompanions.com
Dynamics Companions

- 93 -

www.blindsquirrelpublishing.com
© 2017 Blind Squirrel Publishing, LLC, All Rights Reserved

BLIND SQUIRREL
PUBLISHING

DYNAMICS COMPANIONS
BARE BONES CONFIGURATION GUIDE

CONFIGURING ACCOUNTS PAYABLE WITHIN DYNAMICS 365 FOR OPERATIONS
MODULE 2: CONFIGURING THE ACCOUNTS PAYABLE VENDOR ACCOUNTS

Populating and publishing the Import Template

How to do it...

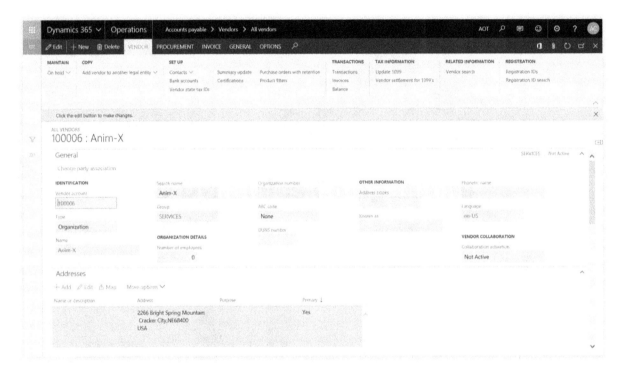

Step 2: Paste in data and click Publish

If we drill into the vendor details we will see all of the data has been loaded.

dyn c
www.dynamicscompanions.com
Dynamics Companions

- 94 -

www.blindsquirrelpublishing.com
© 2017 Blind Squirrel Publishing, LLC, All Rights Reserved

BLIND SQUIRREL
PUBLISHING

DYNAMICS COMPANIONS
BARE BONES CONFIGURATION GUIDE

CONFIGURING ACCOUNTS PAYABLE WITHIN DYNAMICS 365 FOR OPERATIONS
MODULE 2: CONFIGURING THE ACCOUNTS PAYABLE VENDOR ACCOUNTS

Populating and publishing the Import Template

Review

While adding vendors by hand does give you a sense of accomplishment, importing in thousands of vendors without having to do them one by one gives you a sense of achievement.

DYNAMICS COMPANIONS
BARE BONES CONFIGURATION GUIDE

CONFIGURING ACCOUNTS PAYABLE WITHIN DYNAMICS 365 FOR OPERATIONS
MODULE 2: CONFIGURING THE ACCOUNTS PAYABLE VENDOR ACCOUNTS

Updating Vendor Information Manually

Once you have the vendors loaded in, you may want to make a couple of tweaks to them just to polish up the data. One of the ways you can do this is through the vendor details form itself.

How to do it...

Step 1: Open the All vendors form

To do this we will want to go to the **All vendors** form.

Navigate to Accounts Payable > Vendors > All vendors

Step 2: Select a Vendor

All we will need to do here is to open up the vendor record that we want to modify.

Select a **Vendor** record

Sometimes the form will be in read mode, so we will want to switch to the **Edit** mode so that we can make changes to the record.

Step 3: Change the Group code

If the **Group** that is assigned to the vendor is incorrect then we can easily make that change.

Click on the **Group** drop-down list and select the **PARTS** code

Step 4: Change the Language code

Also, we can change is the **Language** code that is assigned to the vendor.

Click on the Language drop-down list and select us-eng (English (United States))

Step 5: Press CTRL+S and exit the form

After we have made the changes that you want to the vendor record we can save the record and then exit from the form.

Press **CTRL+S** to save the record and click on the **X** button.

DYNAMICS COMPANIONS
BARE BONES CONFIGURATION GUIDE

CONFIGURING ACCOUNTS PAYABLE WITHIN DYNAMICS 365 FOR OPERATIONS
MODULE 2: CONFIGURING THE ACCOUNTS PAYABLE VENDOR ACCOUNTS

Updating Vendor Information Manually

How to do it...

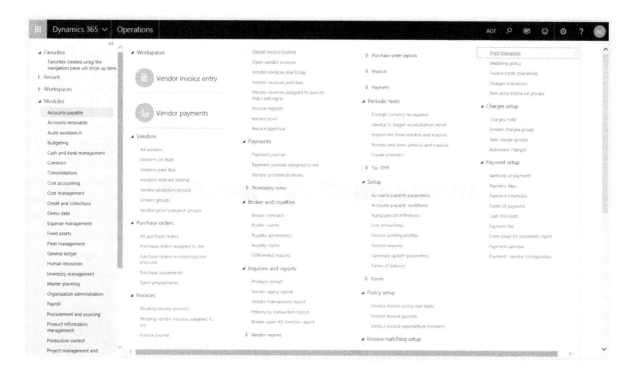

Step 1: Open the All vendors form

To do this we will want to go to the **All vendors** form.

To do this, open up the navigation panel, expand out the **Modules** group, and click on **Accounts payable** module to see all of the menu items that are available. Then click on the **All vendors** menu item within the **Vendors** menu group.

dyn c
www.dynamicscompanions.com
Dynamics Companions

- 97 -

www.blindsquirrelpublishing.com
© 2017 Blind Squirrel Publishing, LLC, All Rights Reserved

BLIND SQUIRREL
PUBLISHING

DYNAMICS COMPANIONS
BARE BONES CONFIGURATION GUIDE

CONFIGURING ACCOUNTS PAYABLE WITHIN DYNAMICS 365 FOR OPERATIONS
MODULE 2: CONFIGURING THE ACCOUNTS PAYABLE VENDOR ACCOUNTS

Updating Vendor Information Manually

How to do it...

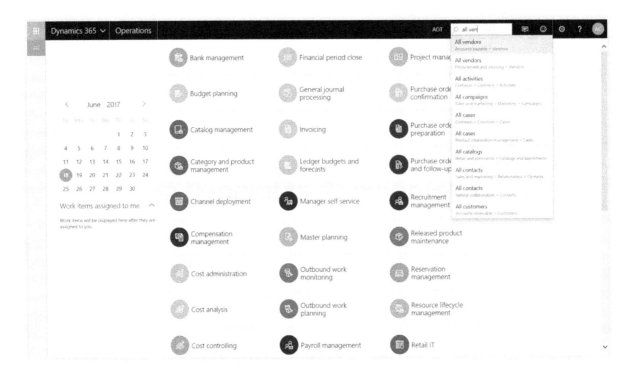

Step 1: Open the All vendors form

Alternatively, you can search for the **All vendors** form by clicking on the search icon in the header of the form (or press **ALT+G)** and then type in **all ven** into the search box. Then you will be able to select the **All vendors** maintenance form from the dropdown list.

dync
www.dynamicscompanions.com
Dynamics Companions

- 98 -

www.blindsquirrelpublishing.com
© 2017 Blind Squirrel Publishing, LLC, All Rights Reserved

BLIND SQUIRREL
PUBLISHING

DYNAMICS COMPANIONS
BARE BONES CONFIGURATION GUIDE

CONFIGURING ACCOUNTS PAYABLE WITHIN DYNAMICS 365 FOR OPERATIONS
MODULE 2: CONFIGURING THE ACCOUNTS PAYABLE VENDOR ACCOUNTS

Updating Vendor Information Manually

How to do it...

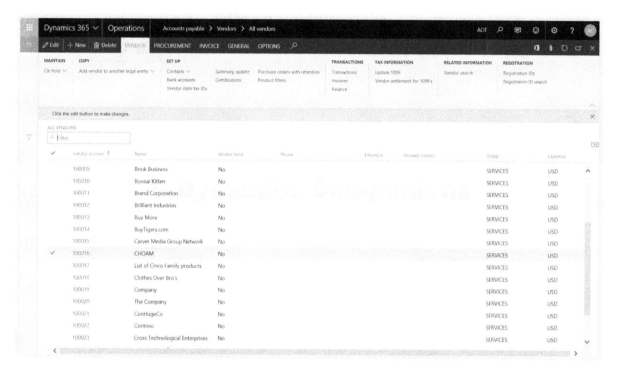

Step 2: Select a Vendor

This will open up the **All vendors** list page where we can see all of the vendor records.

All we will need to do here is to open up the vendor record that we want to modify.

To do this, just pick a vendor and double click on the line in the list page.

For this example we selected **Vendor 100016 (CHOAM)**.

dync
www.dynamicscompanions.com
Dynamics Companions

- 99 -

www.blindsquirrelpublishing.com
© 2017 Blind Squirrel Publishing, LLC, All Rights Reserved

BLIND SQUIRREL
PUBLISHING

DYNAMICS COMPANIONS
BARE BONES CONFIGURATION GUIDE

CONFIGURING ACCOUNTS PAYABLE WITHIN DYNAMICS 365 FOR OPERATIONS
MODULE 2: CONFIGURING THE ACCOUNTS PAYABLE VENDOR ACCOUNTS

Updating Vendor Information Manually

How to do it...

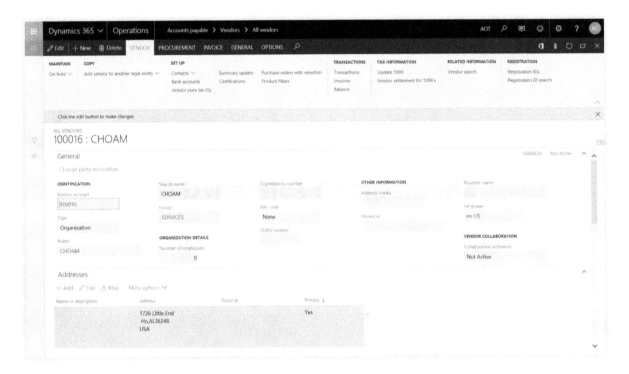

Step 2: Select a Vendor

This will open up the vendor details for us and we will be able to see all of the vendor details.

www.dynamicscompanions.com
Dynamics Companions

- 100 -

www.blindsquirrelpublishing.com
© 2017 Blind Squirrel Publishing, LLC, All Rights Reserved

BLIND SQUIRREL
PUBLISHING

DYNAMICS COMPANIONS
BARE BONES CONFIGURATION GUIDE

CONFIGURING ACCOUNTS PAYABLE WITHIN DYNAMICS 365 FOR OPERATIONS
MODULE 2: CONFIGURING THE ACCOUNTS PAYABLE VENDOR ACCOUNTS

Updating Vendor Information Manually

How to do it...

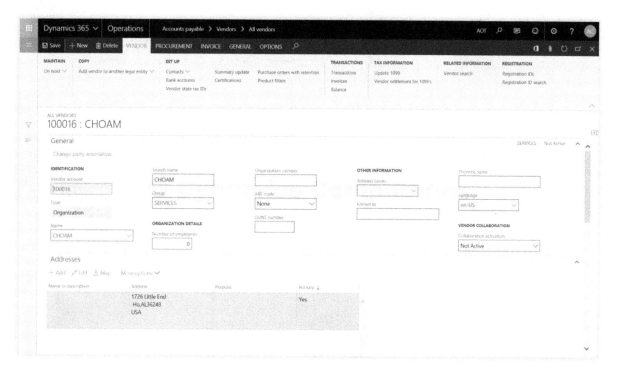

Step 2: Select a Vendor

Sometimes the form will be in read mode, so we will want to switch to the **Edit** mode so that we can make changes to the record.

To do this, just click on the **Edit** button within the menu bar.

This will change the display from read to edit mode and we will see that all of the editable fields are now editable.

DYNAMICS COMPANIONS
BARE BONES CONFIGURATION GUIDE

CONFIGURING ACCOUNTS PAYABLE WITHIN DYNAMICS 365 FOR OPERATIONS
MODULE 2: CONFIGURING THE ACCOUNTS PAYABLE VENDOR ACCOUNTS

Updating Vendor Information Manually

How to do it...

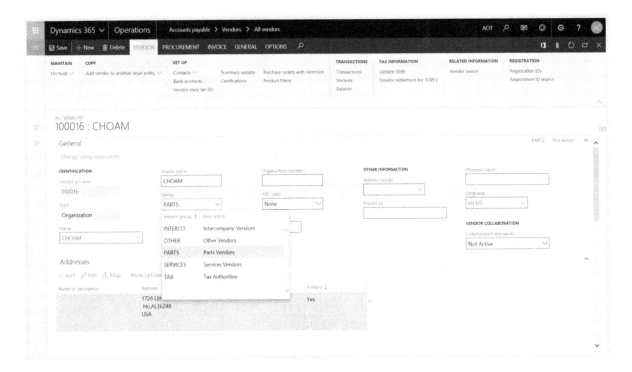

Step 3: Change the Group code

Now we can update any of the fields on the vendor record.

If the **Group** that is assigned to the vendor is incorrect then we can easily make that change.

To do this, just click on the drop-down list for the **Group** field and select the new vendor group.

In this example, we want to change the vendor group to a parts vendor so we clicked on the **Group** drop-down list and select the **PARTS** code from the list

www.dynamicscompanions.com
Dynamics Companions

- 102 -

www.blindsquirrelpublishing.com
© 2017 Blind Squirrel Publishing, LLC, All Rights Reserved

BLIND SQUIRREL
PUBLISHING

DYNAMICS COMPANIONS
BARE BONES CONFIGURATION GUIDE

CONFIGURING ACCOUNTS PAYABLE WITHIN DYNAMICS 365 FOR OPERATIONS
MODULE 2: CONFIGURING THE ACCOUNTS PAYABLE VENDOR ACCOUNTS

Updating Vendor Information Manually

How to do it...

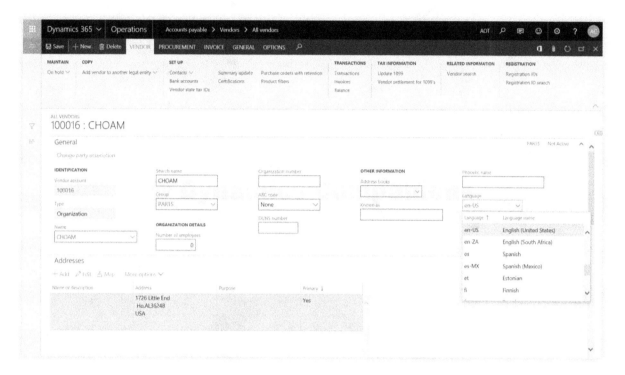

Step 4: Change the Language code

Also, we can change is the **Language** code that is assigned to the vendor.

To do this, just click on the drop-down list for the **Language** field and select the new default language for the vendor.

For this vendor we want the default language to be US English so we clicked on the **Language** drop-down list and selected **us-eng (English (United States))**

dyn c
www.dynamicscompanions.com
Dynamics Companions
- 103 -
www.blindsquirrelpublishing.com
© 2017 Blind Squirrel Publishing, LLC, All Rights Reserved
BLIND SQUIRREL
PUBLISHING

DYNAMICS COMPANIONS
BARE BONES CONFIGURATION GUIDE

CONFIGURING ACCOUNTS PAYABLE WITHIN DYNAMICS 365 FOR OPERATIONS
MODULE 2: CONFIGURING THE ACCOUNTS PAYABLE VENDOR ACCOUNTS

Updating Vendor Information Manually

How to do it...

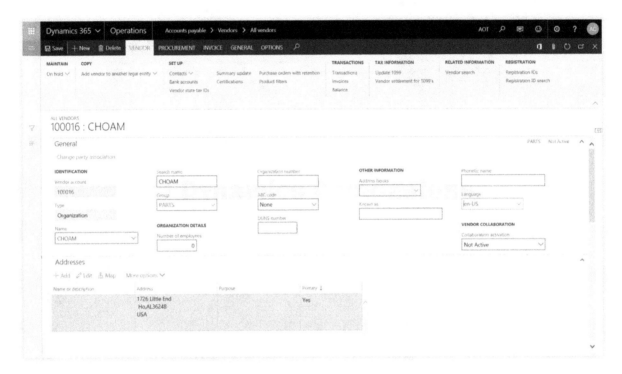

Step 5: Press CTRL+S and exit the form

After we have made the changes that you want to the vendor record we can save the record and then exit from the form.

To do this, just press **CTRL+S** to save the record and then click on the **X** button to exit from the form.

www.dynamicscompanions.com
Dynamics Companions

- 104 -

www.blindsquirrelpublishing.com
© 2017 Blind Squirrel Publishing, LLC, All Rights Reserved

BLIND SQUIRREL
PUBLISHING

DYNAMICS COMPANIONS
BARE BONES CONFIGURATION GUIDE

CONFIGURING ACCOUNTS PAYABLE WITHIN DYNAMICS 365 FOR OPERATIONS
MODULE 2: CONFIGURING THE ACCOUNTS PAYABLE VENDOR ACCOUNTS

Updating Vendor Information Manually

Review

Making small changes to the **Vendor** records is pretty darn simple.

 www.dynamicscompanions.com
Dynamics Companions

- 105 -

www.blindsquirrelpublishing.com
© 2017 Blind Squirrel Publishing, LLC, All Rights Reserved

BLIND SQUIRREL
PUBLISHING

DYNAMICS COMPANIONS
BARE BONES CONFIGURATION GUIDE

CONFIGURING ACCOUNTS PAYABLE WITHIN DYNAMICS 365 FOR OPERATIONS
MODULE 2: CONFIGURING THE ACCOUNTS PAYABLE VENDOR ACCOUNTS

Performing Bulk Updates Using the Grid Editing Feature

Another way that you can make updates to the data is through the **Grid** feature that is built into the vendor maintenance form.

How to do it...

Step 1: Open the All Vendors form

To do this we will want to go to the **All vendors** form.

Navigate to Accounts Payable > Vendors > All vendors

Step 2: Right-mouse-click on any of the fields and select Personalize

If you want to update fields that are not already on the grid, then we can add them to the grid.

Right-mouse-click on any of the fields and select the **Personalize** menu item.

Step 3: Click Personalize this form

Click on the **Personalize this form** button.

From here we can add additional fields to the grid.

Click on the + button.

Step 4: Click on the table grid

Now we need to select the grid that we want to add our fields to.

Click on the table grid.

Step 5: Select a field and click Insert

Now we will add a few more fields to the grid.

Select the **Language** field and then click on the **Insert** button.

Step 6: Click Close

Click on the **Close** button

Step 7: Change the Language

Now we can start updating the record, including the new field that we just added.

Change the **Language** to **us-en**

 www.dynamicscompanions.com
Dynamics Companions

- 106 -

www.blindsquirrelpublishing.com
© 2017 Blind Squirrel Publishing, LLC, All Rights Reserved

BLIND SQUIRREL
PUBLISHING

DYNAMICS COMPANIONS
BARE BONES CONFIGURATION GUIDE

CONFIGURING ACCOUNTS PAYABLE WITHIN DYNAMICS 365 FOR OPERATIONS
MODULE 2: CONFIGURING THE ACCOUNTS PAYABLE VENDOR ACCOUNTS

Performing Bulk Updates Using the Grid Editing Feature

How to do it...

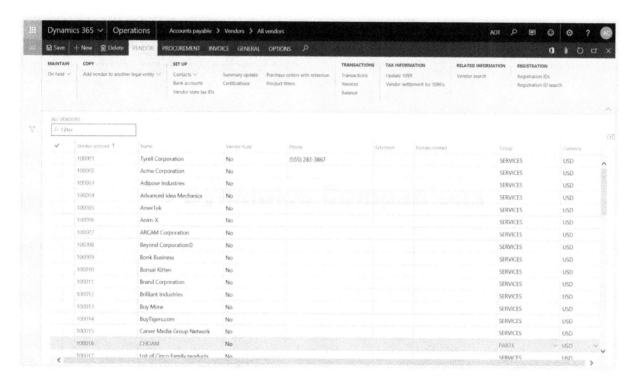

Step 1: Open the All Vendors form

To do this we will want to go to the **All vendors** form.

To do this, open up the **All Vendors** list page.

This will open up the vendors in a new view that acts more like a spreadsheet.

dync
www.dynamicscompanions.com
Dynamics Companions
- 107 -
www.blindsquirrelpublishing.com
© 2017 Blind Squirrel Publishing, LLC , All Rights Reserved
BLIND SQUIRREL
PUBLISHING

DYNAMICS COMPANIONS
BARE BONES CONFIGURATION GUIDE

CONFIGURING ACCOUNTS PAYABLE WITHIN DYNAMICS 365 FOR OPERATIONS
MODULE 2: CONFIGURING THE ACCOUNTS PAYABLE VENDOR ACCOUNTS

Performing Bulk Updates Using the Grid Editing Feature

How to do it...

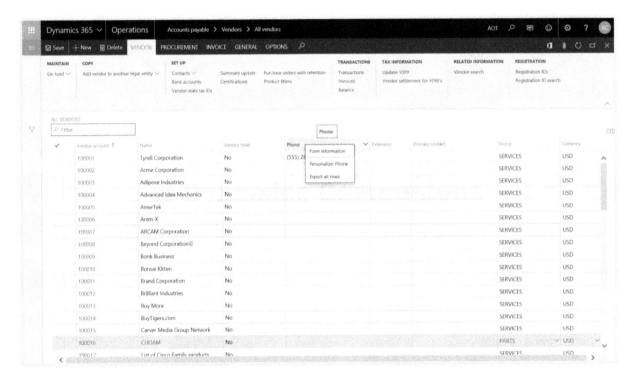

Step 2: Right-mouse-click on any of the fields and select Personalize

If you want to update fields that are not already on the grid, then we can add them to the grid.

To do this, right-mouse-click on any of the fields and select the **Personalize** menu item.

www.dynamicscompanions.com
Dynamics Companions

- 108 -

www.blindsquirrelpublishing.com
© 2017 Blind Squirrel Publishing, LLC, All Rights Reserved

BLIND SQUIRREL
PUBLISHING

DYNAMICS COMPANIONS
BARE BONES CONFIGURATION GUIDE

CONFIGURING ACCOUNTS PAYABLE WITHIN DYNAMICS 365 FOR OPERATIONS
MODULE 2: CONFIGURING THE ACCOUNTS PAYABLE VENDOR ACCOUNTS

Performing Bulk Updates Using the Grid Editing Feature

How to do it...

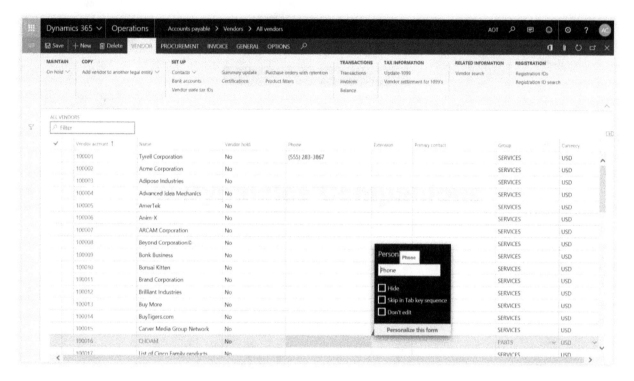

Step 3: Click Personalize this form

This will open up the **Personalize** popup box where we can manipulate the fields, but to do more we can add additional fields.

To do this, click on the **Personalize this form** button.

dync
www.dynamicscompanions.com
Dynamics Companions

- 109 -

www.blindsquirrelpublishing.com
© 2017 Blind Squirrel Publishing, LLC, All Rights Reserved

BLIND SQUIRREL
PUBLISHING

DYNAMICS COMPANIONS
BARE BONES CONFIGURATION GUIDE

CONFIGURING ACCOUNTS PAYABLE WITHIN DYNAMICS 365 FOR OPERATIONS
MODULE 2: CONFIGURING THE ACCOUNTS PAYABLE VENDOR ACCOUNTS

Performing Bulk Updates Using the Grid Editing Feature

How to do it...

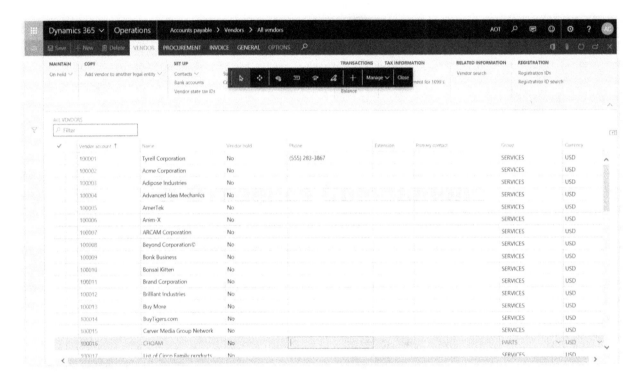

Step 3: Click Personalize this form

This will open up the **Personalization** palette.

From here we can add additional fields to the grid.

To do this, click on the **+** button.

dyn c
www.dynamicscompanions.com
Dynamics Companions

- 110 -

www.blindsquirrelpublishing.com
© 2017 Blind Squirrel Publishing, LLC, All Rights Reserved

BLIND SQUIRREL
PUBLISHING

DYNAMICS COMPANIONS
BARE BONES CONFIGURATION GUIDE

CONFIGURING ACCOUNTS PAYABLE WITHIN DYNAMICS 365 FOR OPERATIONS
MODULE 2: CONFIGURING THE ACCOUNTS PAYABLE VENDOR ACCOUNTS

Performing Bulk Updates Using the Grid Editing Feature

How to do it...

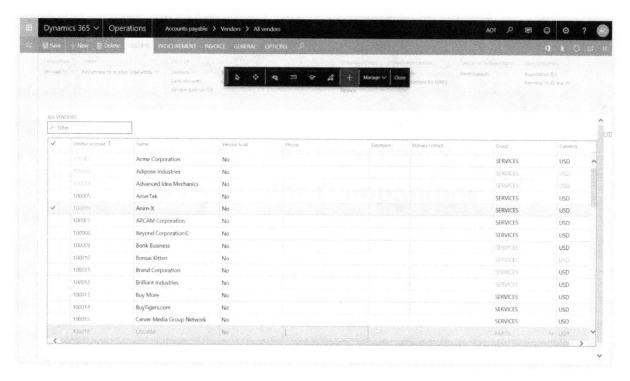

Step 4: Click on the table grid

Now we need to select the grid that we want to add our fields to.

To do this, just select the grid itself that you want to add additional fields to.

www.dynamicscompanions.com
Dynamics Companions

- 111 -

www.blindsquirrelpublishing.com
© 2017 Blind Squirrel Publishing, LLC, All Rights Reserved

BLIND SQUIRREL
PUBLISHING

DYNAMICS COMPANIONS
BARE BONES CONFIGURATION GUIDE

CONFIGURING ACCOUNTS PAYABLE WITHIN DYNAMICS 365 FOR OPERATIONS
MODULE 2: CONFIGURING THE ACCOUNTS PAYABLE VENDOR ACCOUNTS

Performing Bulk Updates Using the Grid Editing Feature

How to do it...

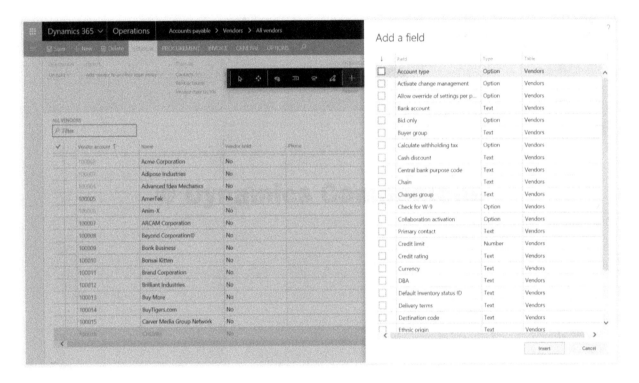

Step 4: Click on the table grid

This will open up the field explorer and we can add any field from the main **Vendor** table and also any of the related tables to the grid.

www.dynamicscompanions.com
Dynamics Companions

- 112 -

www.blindsquirrelpublishing.com
© 2017 Blind Squirrel Publishing, LLC, All Rights Reserved

BLIND SQUIRREL
PUBLISHING

DYNAMICS COMPANIONS
BARE BONES CONFIGURATION GUIDE

CONFIGURING ACCOUNTS PAYABLE WITHIN DYNAMICS 365 FOR OPERATIONS
MODULE 2: CONFIGURING THE ACCOUNTS PAYABLE VENDOR ACCOUNTS

Performing Bulk Updates Using the Grid Editing Feature

How to do it...

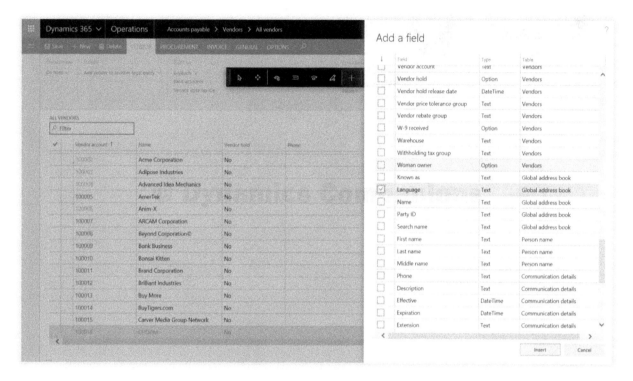

Step 5: Select a field and click Insert

Now we will add a few more fields to the grid.

All we need to do is just select the **Field** that we want to add to the form and then click on the **Add** button.

For example, if you open up the **Global Address Book** group then you will be able to select the **Language** field and then click on the **Insert** button to add it to the grid.

www.dynamicscompanions.com
Dynamics Companions

- 113 -

www.blindsquirrelpublishing.com
© 2017 Blind Squirrel Publishing, LLC, All Rights Reserved

BLIND SQUIRREL
PUBLISHING

DYNAMICS COMPANIONS
BARE BONES CONFIGURATION GUIDE

CONFIGURING ACCOUNTS PAYABLE WITHIN DYNAMICS 365 FOR OPERATIONS
MODULE 2: CONFIGURING THE ACCOUNTS PAYABLE VENDOR ACCOUNTS

Performing Bulk Updates Using the Grid Editing Feature

How to do it...

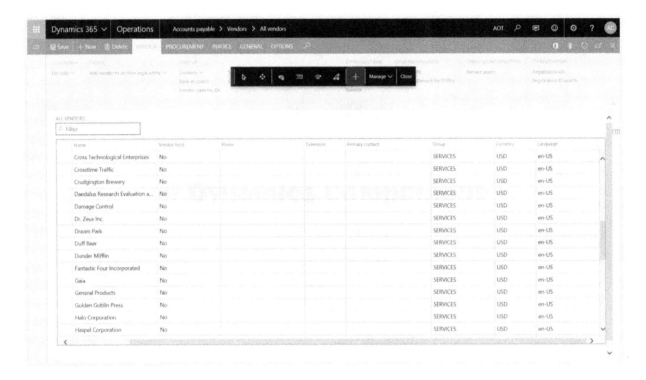

Step 6: Click Close

Now the grid will have the new fields that you added.

To return back to edit mode, click on the **Close** button.

dyn c
www.dynamicscompanions.com
Dynamics Companions

- 114 -

www.blindsquirrelpublishing.com
© 2017 Blind Squirrel Publishing, LLC, All Rights Reserved

BLIND SQUIRREL
PUBLISHING

DYNAMICS COMPANIONS
BARE BONES CONFIGURATION GUIDE

CONFIGURING ACCOUNTS PAYABLE WITHIN DYNAMICS 365 FOR OPERATIONS
MODULE 2: CONFIGURING THE ACCOUNTS PAYABLE VENDOR ACCOUNTS

Performing Bulk Updates Using the Grid Editing Feature

How to do it...

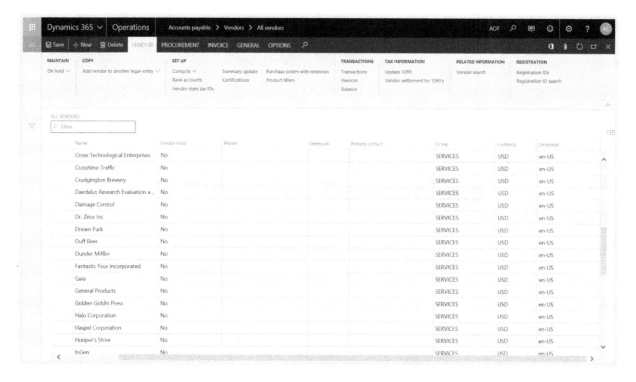

Step 6: Click Close

When you return to the grid page you will see that the **Language** field has been added.

www.dynamicscompanions.com
Dynamics Companions

- 115 -

www.blindsquirrelpublishing.com
© 2017 Blind Squirrel Publishing, LLC, All Rights Reserved

BLIND SQUIRREL
PUBLISHING

DYNAMICS COMPANIONS
BARE BONES CONFIGURATION GUIDE

CONFIGURING ACCOUNTS PAYABLE WITHIN DYNAMICS 365 FOR OPERATIONS
MODULE 2: CONFIGURING THE ACCOUNTS PAYABLE VENDOR ACCOUNTS

Performing Bulk Updates Using the Grid Editing Feature

How to do it...

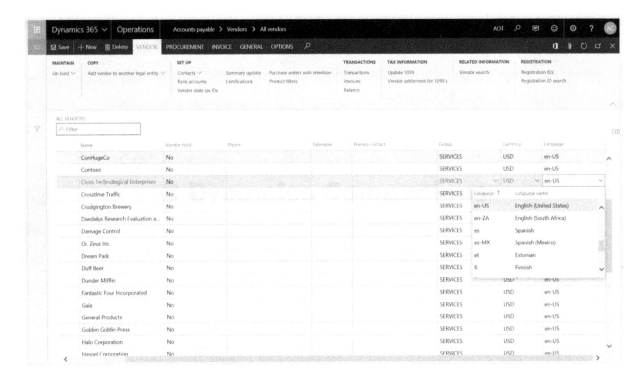

Step 7: Change the Language

Now we can start updating the record, including the new field that we just added.

To do this, just select the field and update it within the grid.

For example, we selected the **100017** vendor and changed the **Language** to **en-us.**

DYNAMICS COMPANIONS
BARE BONES CONFIGURATION GUIDE

CONFIGURING ACCOUNTS PAYABLE WITHIN DYNAMICS 365 FOR OPERATIONS
MODULE 2: CONFIGURING THE ACCOUNTS PAYABLE VENDOR ACCOUNTS

Performing Bulk Updates Using the Grid Editing Feature

How to do it...

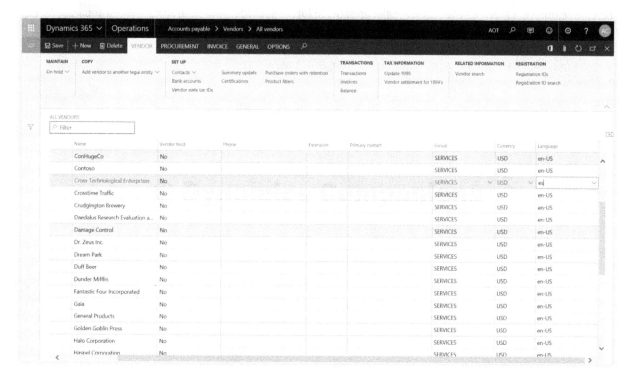

Step 7: Change the Language

You can use the arrow keys to move through the records and update multiple fields.

That is too easy.

BLIND SQUIRREL
PUBLISHING

DYNAMICS COMPANIONS
BARE BONES CONFIGURATION GUIDE

CONFIGURING ACCOUNTS PAYABLE WITHIN DYNAMICS 365 FOR OPERATIONS
MODULE 2: CONFIGURING THE ACCOUNTS PAYABLE VENDOR ACCOUNTS

Performing Bulk Updates Using the Grid Editing Feature

Review

The **Grid** feature is a great way to quickly make updates to lots of records. And also, since this is a separate form, then you can have two views onto the vendor record to make it easier to view and also manage the records.

DYNAMICS COMPANIONS
BARE BONES CONFIGURATION GUIDE

CONFIGURING ACCOUNTS PAYABLE WITHIN DYNAMICS 365 FOR OPERATIONS
MODULE 2: CONFIGURING THE ACCOUNTS PAYABLE VENDOR ACCOUNTS

Performing Mass Updates Using Excel

Sometimes, if you have a lot of records to update you may want to use Excel as your maintenance tool.

How to do it...

Step 1: Click Open In Excel

The office integration allows us to open the **Vendors** entity within Excel directly from the form.

Click on the Office integration icon, and then select the **Open in Excel** template.

Step 2: Click Download

We will open the workbook locally.

Click on the **Download** button.

Step 3: Click Open

Here we will want to open up the Excel workbook.

Click on the **Open** button.

Step 4: Click Enable editing

The worksheet will be in read only mode right now.

Click on the **Enable editing** button

Step 5: Click on the Vendor hold cell

Click on the **Vendor hold** cell.

Step 6: Change the Vendor hold

Within the Excel spreadsheet we can change the values.

Change the Vendor hold to Payment

Step 7: Click Publish

Once we have made our changes we can publish the data back to Dynamics.

Click on the **Publish** menu button

www.dynamicscompanions.com
Dynamics Companions

- 119 -

www.blindsquirrelpublishing.com
© 2017 Blind Squirrel Publishing, LLC, All Rights Reserved

BLIND SQUIRREL
PUBLISHING

DYNAMICS COMPANIONS
BARE BONES CONFIGURATION GUIDE

CONFIGURING ACCOUNTS PAYABLE WITHIN DYNAMICS 365 FOR OPERATIONS
MODULE 2: CONFIGURING THE ACCOUNTS PAYABLE VENDOR ACCOUNTS

Performing Mass Updates Using Excel

How to do it...

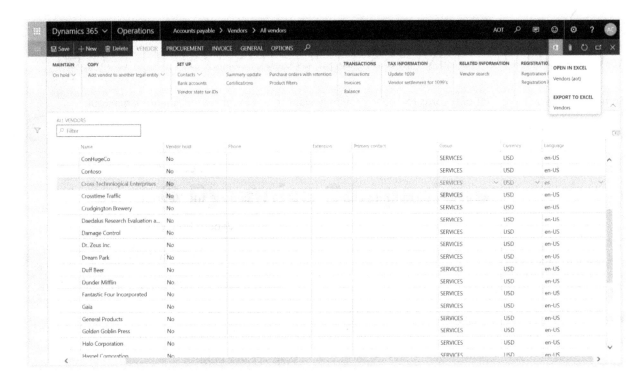

Step 1: Click Open In Excel

The office integration allows us to open the **Vendors** entity within Excel directly from the form.

There are two different options with the Office integration.

Open in Excel: This opens up the data within excel as a live connection, allowing you to make changes to the records and then publish them back to Dynamics.

Export to Excel: This option will open up a copy of the data in excel with no link back to the database.

To open the Vendors data in Excel, just click on the Office integration icon, and then select the **Open in Excel** template.

For this example we will select the **Vendors (aot)** template.

dyn c
www.dynamicscompanions.com
Dynamics Companions

- 120 -

www.blindsquirrelpublishing.com
© 2017 Blind Squirrel Publishing, LLC, All Rights Reserved

BLIND SQUIRREL
PUBLISHING

DYNAMICS COMPANIONS
BARE BONES CONFIGURATION GUIDE

CONFIGURING ACCOUNTS PAYABLE WITHIN DYNAMICS 365 FOR OPERATIONS
MODULE 2: CONFIGURING THE ACCOUNTS PAYABLE VENDOR ACCOUNTS

Performing Mass Updates Using Excel

How to do it...

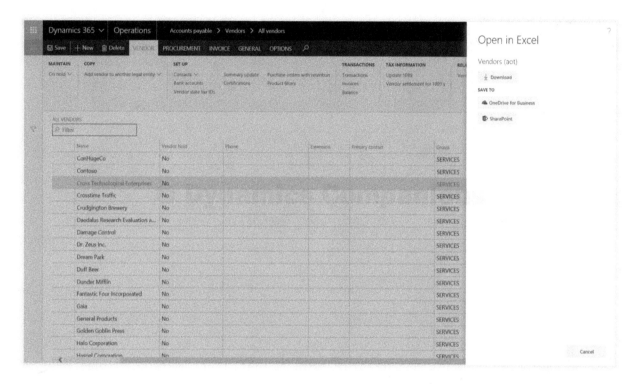

Step 2: Click Download

This will open up a dialog panel that asks us where we want to open up the Excel workbook.

We will open the workbook locally.

To do this, just click on the **Download** button.

dync
www.dynamicscompanions.com
Dynamics Companions

- 121 -

www.blindsquirrelpublishing.com
© 2017 Blind Squirrel Publishing, LLC, All Rights Reserved

BLIND SQUIRREL
PUBLISHING

DYNAMICS COMPANIONS
BARE BONES CONFIGURATION GUIDE

CONFIGURING ACCOUNTS PAYABLE WITHIN DYNAMICS 365 FOR OPERATIONS
MODULE 2: CONFIGURING THE ACCOUNTS PAYABLE VENDOR ACCOUNTS

Performing Mass Updates Using Excel

How to do it...

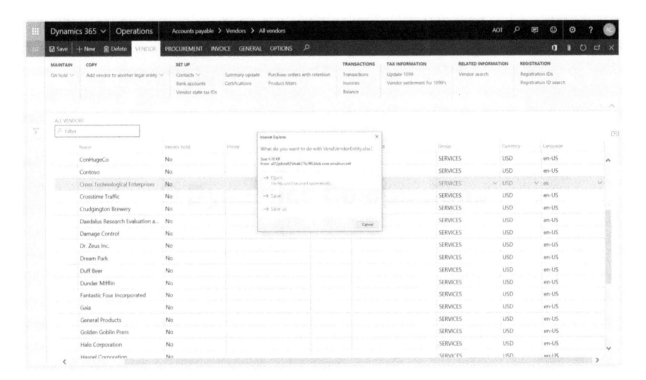

Step 3: Click Open

This will cause an explorer dialog box to be displayed.

Here we will want to open up the Excel workbook.

To do this, just click on the **Open** button.

www.dynamicscompanions.com
Dynamics Companions

- 122 -

www.blindsquirrelpublishing.com
© 2017 Blind Squirrel Publishing, LLC, All Rights Reserved

BLIND SQUIRREL
PUBLISHING

DYNAMICS COMPANIONS
BARE BONES CONFIGURATION GUIDE

CONFIGURING ACCOUNTS PAYABLE WITHIN DYNAMICS 365 FOR OPERATIONS
MODULE 2: CONFIGURING THE ACCOUNTS PAYABLE VENDOR ACCOUNTS

Performing Mass Updates Using Excel

How to do it...

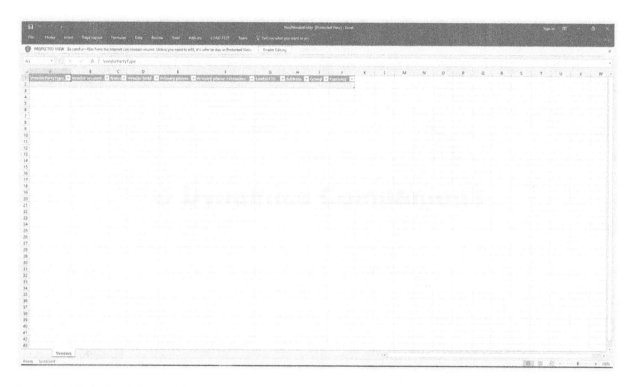

Step 4: Click Enable editing

Next thing you know, Excel will open up and we will see all of the fields that we selected from the entity are showing up as columns.

The worksheet will be in read only mode right now.

To activate the worksheet, we just need to click on the **Enable editing** button in the message bar.

www.dynamicscompanions.com
Dynamics Companions
- 123 -
www.blindsquirrelpublishing.com
© 2017 Blind Squirrel Publishing, LLC, All Rights Reserved
BLIND SQUIRREL PUBLISHING

DYNAMICS COMPANIONS
BARE BONES CONFIGURATION GUIDE

CONFIGURING ACCOUNTS PAYABLE WITHIN DYNAMICS 365 FOR OPERATIONS
MODULE 2: CONFIGURING THE ACCOUNTS PAYABLE VENDOR ACCOUNTS

Performing Mass Updates Using Excel

How to do it...

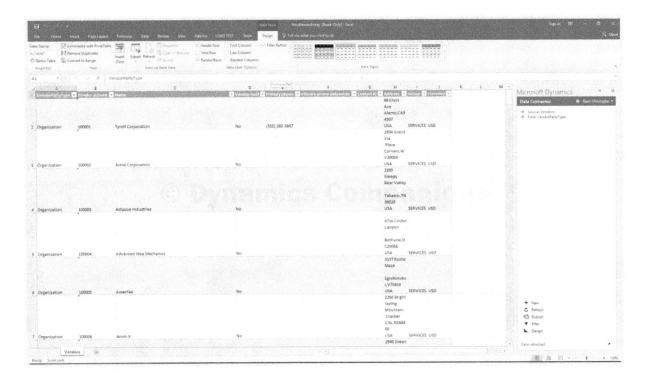

Step 4: Click Enable editing

This will open up a new Excel panel for the integration to Dynamics 365, and also populate the worksheet with all of the existing data. There isn't much right now, but in the next section we will fix that.

dyn c
www.dynamicscompanions.com
Dynamics Companions

- 124 -

www.blindsquirrelpublishing.com
© 2017 Blind Squirrel Publishing, LLC, All Rights Reserved

BLIND SQUIRREL
PUBLISHING

DYNAMICS COMPANIONS
BARE BONES CONFIGURATION GUIDE

CONFIGURING ACCOUNTS PAYABLE WITHIN DYNAMICS 365 FOR OPERATIONS
MODULE 2: CONFIGURING THE ACCOUNTS PAYABLE VENDOR ACCOUNTS

Performing Mass Updates Using Excel

How to do it...

Step 5: Click on the Vendor hold cell

From within the Excel worksheet we can now select any of the cells and if there are reference tables linked to the field then the different values will show up in the Dynamics 365 data panel.

To see this in action, just click on the **Vendor hold** cell.

dyn c
www.dynamicscompanions.com
Dynamics Companions

- 125 -

www.blindsquirrelpublishing.com
© 2017 Blind Squirrel Publishing, LLC, All Rights Reserved

BLIND SQUIRREL
PUBLISHING

DYNAMICS COMPANIONS
BARE BONES CONFIGURATION GUIDE

CONFIGURING ACCOUNTS PAYABLE WITHIN DYNAMICS 365 FOR OPERATIONS
MODULE 2: CONFIGURING THE ACCOUNTS PAYABLE VENDOR ACCOUNTS

Performing Mass Updates Using Excel

How to do it...

Step 6: Change the Vendor hold

Within the Excel spreadsheet we can change the values.

To do this, just change the value in the cell.

www.dynamicscompanions.com
Dynamics Companions

- 126 -

www.blindsquirrelpublishing.com
© 2017 Blind Squirrel Publishing, LLC, All Rights Reserved

BLIND SQUIRREL
PUBLISHING

DYNAMICS COMPANIONS
BARE BONES CONFIGURATION GUIDE

CONFIGURING ACCOUNTS PAYABLE WITHIN DYNAMICS 365 FOR OPERATIONS
MODULE 2: CONFIGURING THE ACCOUNTS PAYABLE VENDOR ACCOUNTS

Performing Mass Updates Using Excel

How to do it...

Step 7: Click Publish

Once we have made our changes we can publish the data back to Dynamics.

To do this we just need to click on the **Publish** button in the Excel panel.

Now the record within Dynamics will be updated.

www.dynamicscompanions.com
Dynamics Companions

- 127 -

www.blindsquirrelpublishing.com
© 2017 Blind Squirrel Publishing, LLC, All Rights Reserved

BLIND SQUIRREL
PUBLISHING

DYNAMICS COMPANIONS
BARE BONES CONFIGURATION GUIDE

CONFIGURING ACCOUNTS PAYABLE WITHIN DYNAMICS 365 FOR OPERATIONS
MODULE 2: CONFIGURING THE ACCOUNTS PAYABLE VENDOR ACCOUNTS

Performing Mass Updates Using Excel

Review

Although the Grid feature is pretty easy to use, we have to admit that making changes to records through Excel is an even better option because we can use the full power of Excel to craft our changes.

If we want to create formulas as templates to help us work out what we want to update then that's easy to do. Also, the copy and paste functions within Excel are a lot more powerful as well.

DYNAMICS COMPANIONS
BARE BONES CONFIGURATION GUIDE

CONFIGURING ACCOUNTS PAYABLE WITHIN DYNAMICS 365 FOR OPERATIONS
MODULE 2: CONFIGURING THE ACCOUNTS PAYABLE VENDOR ACCOUNTS

Summary

Congratulations. We are now experts in creating and maintaining vendor records. And because we also know how to import in the records from excel files, loading in all of our records is a breeze.

Now that we have vendors in our system, we can start moving on to doing something with them.

www.dynamicscompanions.com
Dynamics Companions

- 129 -

www.blindsquirrelpublishing.com
© 2017 Blind Squirrel Publishing, LLC , All Rights Reserved

BLIND SQUIRREL
PUBLISHING

DYNAMICS COMPANIONS
BARE BONES CONFIGURATION GUIDE

CONFIGURING ACCOUNTS PAYABLE WITHIN DYNAMICS 365 FOR OPERATIONS
MODULE 2: CONFIGURING THE ACCOUNTS PAYABLE VENDOR ACCOUNTS

About The Author

Murray Fife is an Author of over 20 books on Microsoft Dynamics including the Bare Bones Configuration Guide series. These guides comprise of over 15 books which step you through the setup and configuration of Microsoft Dynamics including Finance, Operations, Human Resources, Production, Service Management, and Project Accounting.

Throughout his 25+ years of experience in the software industry he has worked in many different roles during his career, including as a developer, an implementation consultant, a trainer and a demo guy within the partner channel which gives him a great understanding of the requirements for both customers and partners perspective.

If you are interested in contacting Murray or want to follow his blogs and posts then here is all of his contact information:

Email: murray@murrayfife.com

Twitter: @murrayfife
Facebook: facebook.com/murraycfife
Google: google.com/+murrayfife
LinkedIn: linkedin.com/in/murrayfife

Blog: atinkerersnotebook.com
Slideshare: slideshare.net/murrayfife
Amazon: amazon.com/author/murrayfife

dync
www.dynamicscompanions.com
Dynamics Companions

- 131 -

www.blindsquirrelpublishing.com
© 2017 Blind Squirrel Publishing, LLC, All Rights Reserved

BLIND SQUIRREL
PUBLISHING

DYNAMICS COMPANIONS
BARE BONES CONFIGURATION GUIDE

CONFIGURING ACCOUNTS PAYABLE WITHIN DYNAMICS 365 FOR OPERATIONS
MODULE 2: CONFIGURING THE ACCOUNTS PAYABLE VENDOR ACCOUNTS

Need More Help with Microsoft Dynamics AX 2012 or Dynamics 365 for Operations

We are firm believers that Microsoft Dynamics AX 2012 or Dynamics 365 is not a hard product to learn, but the problem is where do you start. Which is why we developed the Bare Bones Configuration Guides. The aim of this series is to step you though the configuration of Microsoft Dynamics from a blank system, and then step you through the setup of all of the core modules within Microsoft Dynamics. We start with the setup of a base system, then move on to the financial, distribution, and operations modules.

Each book builds upon the previous ones, and by the time you have worked through all of the guides then you will have completely configured a simple (but functional) Microsoft Dynamics instance. To make it even more worthwhile you will have a far better understanding of Microsoft Dynamics and also how everything fits together.

As of now there are 16 guides in this series broken out as follows:

- Configuring a Training Environment
- Configuring an Organization
- Configuring the General Ledger
- Configuring Cash and Bank Management
- Configuring Accounts Receivable
- Configuring Accounts Payable
- Configuring Product Information Management
- Configuring Inventory Management

- Configuring Procurement and Sourcing
- Configuring Sales Order Management
- Configuring Human Resource Management
- Configuring Project Management and Accounting
- Configuring Production Control
- Configuring Sales and Marketing
- Configuring Service Management
- Configuring Warehouse Management

Although you can get each of these guides individually, and we think that each one is a great Visual resources to step you through each of the particular modules, for those of you that want to take full advantage of the series, you will want to start from the beginning and work through them one by one. After you have done that you would have done people told me was impossible for one persons to do, and that is to configure all of the core modules within Microsoft Dynamics.

If you are interested in finding out more about the series and also view all of the details including topics covered within the module, then browse to the Bare Bones Configuration Guide landing page on the Microsoft Dynamics Companions website. You will find all of the details, and also downloadable resources that help you with the setup of Microsoft Dynamics. Here is the full link: http://www.dynamicscompanions.com/

dyn<c>
www.dynamicscompanions.com
Dynamics Companions

- 133 -

www.blindsquirrelpublishing.com
© 2017 Blind Squirrel Publishing, LLC, All Rights Reserved

BLIND SQUIRREL
PUBLISHING

DYNAMICS COMPANIONS
BARE BONES CONFIGURATION GUIDE

CONFIGURING ACCOUNTS PAYABLE WITHIN DYNAMICS 365 FOR OPERATIONS
MODULE 2: CONFIGURING THE ACCOUNTS PAYABLE VENDOR ACCOUNTS

Usage Agreement

Blind Squirrel Publishing, LLC (the Publisher) agrees to grant, and the user of the eBook agrees to accept, a nonexclusive license to use the eBook under the terms and conditions of this eBook License Agreement ("Agreement"). Your use of the eBook constitutes your agreement to the terms and conditions set forth in this Agreement. This Agreement, or any part thereof, cannot be changed, waived, or discharged other than by a statement in writing signed by you and Blind Squirrel Publishing, LLC. Please read the entire Agreement carefully.

EBook Usage. The eBook may be used by one user on any device. The user of the eBook shall be subject to all of the terms of this Agreement, whether or not the user was the purchaser.

Printing. You may occasionally print a few pages of the text (but not entire sections), which may include sending the printed pages to a third party in the normal course of your business, but you must warn the recipient in writing that copyright law prohibits the recipient from redistributing the eBook content to anyone else. Other than the above, you may not print pages and/or distribute eBook content to others.

Copyright, Use and Resale Prohibitions. The Publisher retains all rights not expressly granted to you in this Agreement. The software, content, and related documentation in the eBook are protected by copyright laws and international copyright treaties, as well as other intellectual property laws and treaties. Nothing in this Agreement constitutes a waiver of the publisher's rights. The Publisher will not be responsible for performance problems due to circumstances beyond its reasonable control. Other than as stated in this Agreement, you may not copy, print, modify, remove, delete, augment, add to, publish, transmit, sell, resell, license, create derivative works from, or in any way exploit any of the eBook's content, in whole or in part, in print or electronic form, and you may not aid or permit others to do so. The unauthorized use or distribution of copyrighted or other proprietary content is illegal and could subject the purchaser to substantial damages. Purchaser will be liable for any damage resulting from any violation of this Agreement.

No Transfer. This license is not transferable by the eBook purchaser unless such transfer is approved in advance by the Publisher.

Disclaimer. The eBook, or any support given by the Publisher are in no way substitutes for assistance from legal, tax, accounting, or other qualified professionals. If legal advice or other expert assistance is required, the services of a competent professional person should be sought.

Limitation of Liability. The eBook is provided "as is" and the Publisher does not make any warranty or representation, either express or implied, to the eBook, including its quality, accuracy, performance, merchantability, or fitness for a particular purpose. You assume the entire risk as to the results and performance of the eBook. The Publisher does not warrant, guarantee, or make any representations regarding the use of, or the results obtained with, the eBook in terms of accuracy, correctness or reliability. In no event will the Publisher be liable for indirect, special, incidental, or consequential damages arising out of delays, errors, omissions, inaccuracies, or the use or inability to use the eBook, or for interruption of the eBook, from whatever cause. This will apply even if the Publisher has been advised that the possibility of such damage exists. Specifically, the Publisher is not responsible for any costs, including those incurred as a result of lost profits or revenue, loss of data, the cost of recovering such programs or data, the cost of any substitute program, claims by third parties, or similar costs. Except for the Publisher's indemnification obligations in Section 7.2, in no case will the Publisher's liability exceed the amount of license fees paid.

DYNAMICS COMPANIONS
BARE BONES CONFIGURATION GUIDE

CONFIGURING ACCOUNTS PAYABLE WITHIN DYNAMICS 365 FOR OPERATIONS
MODULE 2: CONFIGURING THE ACCOUNTS PAYABLE VENDOR ACCOUNTS

Hold Harmless / Indemnification.

7.1 You agree to defend, indemnify and hold the Publisher and any third party provider harmless from and against all third party claims and damages (including reasonable attorneys' fees) regarding your use of the eBook, unless the claims or damages are due to the Publisher's or any third party provider's gross negligence or willful misconduct or arise out of an allegation for which the Publisher is obligated to indemnify you.

7.The Publisher shall defend, indemnify and hold you harmless at the Publisher's expense in any suit, claim or proceeding brought against you alleging that your use of the eBook delivered to you hereunder directly infringes a United States patent, copyright, trademark, trade secret, or other third party proprietary right, provided the Publisher is (i) promptly notified, (ii) given the assistance required at the Publisher's expense, and (iii) permitted to retain legal counsel of the Publisher's choice and to direct the defense. The Publisher also agrees to pay any damages and costs awarded against you by final judgment of a court of last resort in any such suit or any agreed settlement amount on account of any such alleged infringement, but the Publisher will have no liability for settlements or costs incurred without its consent. Should your use of any such eBook be enjoined, or in the event that the Publisher desires to minimize its liability hereunder, the Publisher will, at its option and expense, (i) substitute a fully equivalent non-infringing eBook for the infringing item; (ii) modify the infringing item so that it no longer infringes but remains substantially equivalent; or (iii) obtain for you the right to continue use of such item. If none of the foregoing is feasible, the Publisher will terminate your access to the eBook and refund to you the applicable fees paid by you for the infringing item(s). THE FOREGOING STATES THE ENTIRE LIABILITY OF THE PUBLISHER AND YOUR SOLE REMEDY FOR INFRINGEMENT OR FOR ANY BREACH OF WARRANTY OF NON-INFRINGEMENT, EXPRESS OR IMPLIED. THIS INDEMNITY WILL NOT APPLY TO ANY ALLEGED INFRINGEMENT BASED UPON A COMBINATION OF OTHER SOFTWARE OR INFORMATION WITH THE EBOOK WHERE THE EBOOK WOULD NOT HAVE OTHERWISE INFRINGED ON ITS OWN.

www.ingramcontent.com/pod-product-compliance
Lightning Source LLC
Chambersburg PA
CBHW080425060326

40689CB00019B/4381